RED BIRD

BY

DIANDRA F WING

ACKNOWLEDGMENT

I want to express my heartfelt gratitude to my close friends and family. Your unwavering support and understanding have been my anchor throughout this writing journey, and I cannot thank you enough for being there every step of the way.

A special thank you to my husband, Ben, whose constant encouragement and belief in my dream kept me motivated. You have been my greatest cheerleader, inspiring me to persevere even when the path felt daunting.

I also want to extend my deepest appreciation to you, the reader. This book has been a dream of mine, and your willingness to embark on this journey with me makes it all the more meaningful. Thank you for being part of this adventure!

AUTHOR'S DEDICATION

Dedicated to the memory of my mother, my beautiful Red Bird. I will love you forever, for always, for the rest of my life and beyond.

ABOUT THE AUTHOR

Diandra Ford-Wing is a dynamic and innovative Sales Director whose profound journey through grief ignited her passion for storytelling. After the sudden loss of her mother, Diandra made the courageous decision to pause her thriving career, allowing herself the space to heal and reflect. This transformative experience ultimately inspired her debut novel, "Red Bird," a heartfelt exploration of loss and resilience.

Growing up as an Army Brat, Diandra's life was defined by constant change and adventure, spending her formative years in diverse locations, including Germany. These rich experiences have deeply influenced her narrative voice, infusing her writing with a unique perspective and cultural depth.

When she's not connecting with clients or weaving captivating tales, Diandra enjoys the simple pleasures of life with her husband, Ben, and their two beloved Doodles, CoCo and XuXa. She finds joy in the balance of her professional and personal worlds, and through her writing, she aspires to resonate with others navigating their own paths of loss and self-discovery. Diandra's journey is a testament to the power of storytelling as a means of healing, and she invites readers to join her on this transformative adventure.

TABLE OF CONTENTS

PREFACE

Zora Neale Hurston once eloquently stated that some years pose questions while others provide answers. For me, 2023 was a year of revelations. It illuminated the intricate tapestry of life, unveiling profound insights about the nature of love and, most poignantly, the depths of loss. To fully embrace the warmth of love, one must also navigate the sharp edges of heartache. This delicate balance captures the essence of savoring both the bitter and the sweet.

In my family, we hold a deep-rooted belief in the significance of signs from the universe—whispers of guidance woven into the fabric of everyday life, waiting for us to open our hearts and minds to receive them. One such sign is the striking presence of a red bird, a vivid splash of color against the backdrop of our struggles, symbolizing hope and positivity. The cardinal, in particular, serves as a reminder of our cherished loved ones who have passed, reassuring us that love is a force that transcends even death.

Though these radiant birds are rare, every time I glimpse one, a wave of gratitude washes over me. In those fleeting moments, I feel my loved ones drawing near, their spirits enveloping me in a comforting embrace, watching over me with boundless love.

Chapter 1

Audrey

The Davis family was a close-knit group, comprised of my mother, Sandra, along with her siblings: Patricia, Jaquelyn, Michael, Tanya, and the youngest, Audrey—who we lovingly referred to as Shawn, a nod to her middle name, LaShawn. Their matriarch, Ruth, and patriarch, Allen, had the privilege of raising their six children in the serene expanses of Albany, Georgia. We affectionately called it "the country," as their home was nestled far beyond the bustling edges of town. This cherished house stood on land originally purchased by my great-great-grandmother, where both she and my great-grandparents built their homes. It created a trifecta of families, allowing the Davis clan to grow up surrounded by their elders, fostering a rich and vibrant upbringing.

Shawn, the baby of the family, was always my favorite. She was savvy, often stirring the pot, and her fiery spirit was sometimes hard for others to grasp. To me, she embodied a kind of rebellion—fearless, intelligent, and breathtakingly beautiful. I admired her tenacity and respected her relentless quest for happiness.

In my eyes, Shawn was the epitome of a free spirit. She lived life on her own terms, speaking her mind with a candor that left no room for doubt about where you stood with her. Her presence was like a breath of fresh air—invigorating yet challenging. As the years went by, her strong-willed nature often led to spirited debates with her sisters, but that was exactly what I cherished about her. She possessed an abundance of passion and determination, capable of turning her dreams into reality.

Shawn yearned to experience the world beyond her familiar surroundings, harboring a deep desire to travel to Africa. When our grandfather, her father, passed away, she saw it as the perfect opportunity to pursue her dreams. Having cared for him until his last months, she finally felt the freedom to embark on her long-awaited adventure. She chose The Gambia, a small yet vibrant country in West Africa, believing that our ancestors were beckoning her. With unwavering resolve, she saved every penny, sold all of her possessions—including her car—and set off on a journey that would forever change her life.

Before she left, she made one final trip to Texas, where my family and I lived. She spent a few weeks with my mom, and I hosted a farewell party for her at my home. Shawn was looking forward to returning in the new year for a dear friend's wedding, but we never saw her alive again. I often wondered why she chose The Gambia, one of the smallest countries in West Africa, surrounded by Senegal on all sides, with the Atlantic Ocean to the west. The country faces extreme poverty, and I struggled to understand her decision. However, as I learned more about its culture, I discovered that the Gambian people are known for their tolerance, and the country is considered one of the most peaceful in the region. While the cost of living is low, so are the salaries. I believed she wanted to make a difference, to be a source of hope for those who had lost it. She loved the proximity to the ocean and often sent us pictures of her walks along the beach, capturing stunning sunsets.

Upon arriving in The Gambia, Shawn quickly purchased land, found a home, and connected with the local villagers, who embraced her vibrant spirit and appreciated her contributions. Shortly after her arrival, she met a man, and within weeks, they were engaged. My mom was cautious about this whirlwind romance, but Shawn's happiness was evident. We speculated that she might have known him before moving, though it was never confirmed. We all wanted her to be happy, even if it meant being with someone she had just met. My mom welcomed him into the family and gave her blessing. The two communicated regularly, as much as the time difference allowed, and everything seemed to be going smoothly as they planned their wedding.

Weeks before they were set to marry, my mom received a frantic 5 a.m. phone call from Shawn's fiancé. Shawn was dead. We didn't know what to make of the story her fiancé recounted through his grief. She had been there for just eight months, and now she was gone. They had gone out earlier that evening, met up with some friends, and had some food and drinks. They retired fairly early, around 10 p.m. Around 2 or 3 a.m., her fiancé awoke to use the restroom. He noticed that Shawn looked a little "funny," but her eyes were closed. He tried to rouse her from her sleep, but she was unresponsive. He threw some water on her face, yet she still did not wake up. The emergency response team arrived and took her to the local hospital in Banjul, but she was pronounced dead.

I made the drive from Austin to Killeen, TX, where my mom lived. I saw a red bird along the way, as the early morning hours turned to dawn. I knew it was Shawn, telling me she was okay, that she had made the trek to Heaven and was beyond tickled to be reunited with her mother. My older sister, Ylencia, who was the one who called me, was already there, trying unsuccessfully to console my mom. I made a beeline to her side and comforted her as best I could. The air was thick with grief. I could feel it emanating from my mom's body as she sat in one of the armchairs, slumped over as if the weight of her pain was too much to bear. I rubbed her back, and Ylencia and I cried with her, for her. We felt as if there wasn't much else we could do to console her.

"Why did she leave me? She left me!" she repeatedly exclaimed. We just cried with her while muttering unintelligible words of solace. My older brother, Terry, and twin sister, Dionne, arrived shortly thereafter, and we all just sat, not saying much of anything.

My mind was racing. Is she really dead? What actually happened? Was her fiancé involved? How do we get her back to the States? Do we all go to The Gambia? What on earth do we do?

We spent most of the day at my mother's side, enveloped in the heavy silence of a Sunday weighed down by grief. I had work the next morning and preferred to arrive early most days, but the routine felt hollow. Even as I sat at my desk, my mind was a whirlpool of sorrow and disbelief, fixated on one thought: "I have to do something." I retreated into my office, seeking peace in solitude, but instead, I found myself drowning in research. What steps must one take when a loved one dies in a distant land? The answer seemed simple: contact the U.S. embassy in the country where they passed. But simplicity quickly unraveled into frustration.

I scoured the internet for the contact number of the U.S. Embassy in The Gambia, my efforts yielding a chaotic array of results. Determined, I created a spreadsheet of every number I could find and began calling each one, my heart pounding with urgency. My mother tried to reach out too, but her phone was blocked from making international calls. After a futile call to Verizon to lift the restriction, she still could not connect. From our perspective, this was a blessing in disguise; she wasn't strong enough to bear this burden. Her baby sister was gone, and in that moment, it felt like there was nothing we could do. So, I took it upon myself to navigate this arduous process.

Finally, after what felt like an eternity of dialing, I was connected with a representative from the embassy named Conor. As we exchanged information, he posed a question that struck me like a lightning bolt: "Do you suspect any foul play?" The thought had flickered in my mind, but I had pushed it away—until now. Conor's inquiry was unsettling yet not unfounded. Shawn had ventured into The Gambia with a fearless spirit, making bold choices that could have drawn unwanted attention. There she was, an American woman alone in a foreign land, her very presence a target.

She had purchased property, a taxi cab, and was planning to open Kinta's Kottage—a sanctuary for women seeking beauty products and essential oils. She had even asked for my help in designing the logo, and I was happy and honored that she sought my assistance. But now, that dream lay shattered, and a wave of sorrow and anger washed over me. Shawn had so many aspirations, so many plans for the future, and now they were extinguished forever. The agony of her sudden departure was compounded by the knowledge that we couldn't see her one last time.

She was so far away, and it felt like the world had conspired to keep us apart in her final moments.

Once Conor and I worked on collecting Shawn's possessions, we had to tackle the business of getting her remains back to the United States. The embassy had no means to participate in this step, so I had to go out on my own to find a company that could help. I ended up connecting with a company based out of Miami that specialized in the repatriation of human remains. Repatriation, I quickly discovered, is the act of recovering the remains of a U.S. citizen who has died abroad. I had never heard of this terminology before and hoped to never have to write, say, or even think about this word again. The repatriation of her remains was all I could think about. Speaking with the repatriation company in Miami, I learned it could cost upwards of fifty thousand dollars. Ultimately, our family decided to have her buried there. It was where she wanted to be. She had sworn seven ways to Sunday that she would never set foot on the soil of Georgia again. There were too many ill feelings and unresolved issues there that she did not care to revisit.

My family, particularly my mom's side, was a complicated tapestry of emotions. Shawn, with her fierce spirit and strong opinions, often clashed with her sisters—everyone but my mom, who eventually came to embrace Shawn's uniqueness. Their bond deepened as they recognized a shared sense of wanderlust and self-awareness. They connected on a spiritual level. Mom had left their family home and traveled the world as a military wife. Shawn came out of the womb a butterfly, longing to roam free. She was simply meant to do great things; she knew she was destined for more. Their connection flourished despite the ongoing tension with their other sisters, which had plagued our family for years. In the end, my mom distanced herself from the chaos, maintaining ties only with Shawn, a few cousins, and her uncle.

As the days passed with no resolution in sight, I received a video call from the coroner's office. They needed me to identify her body. I remember that day clearly; Mom had come down to Austin to visit me, and she told me to take the call in my master bedroom. I watched the video as it scanned her body, up and down. The image of her face, forever in a state of perpetual sleep, will be etched in my memory. It was her. I sent the video to one of my aunts, just to ensure that this was definitively her. Mom refused to view it, but she didn't need to.

This was Shawn.

Ultimately, Shawn was laid to rest in a Christian cemetery, beneath the sprawling branches of a grand tree.

Conor, from the embassy, attended the service. Though he had never met my aunt, he wanted to pay his respects and ensure that she was laid to rest in peace. We were left in a fog of uncertainty. Should we pursue a possible criminal investigation? Where were her belongings? Where was her fiancé? Could he be a person of interest? So many questions lingered, yet our resources felt woefully inadequate to unravel the mystery of her death. The autopsy report revealed fluid in her lungs, concluding that she had succumbed to heart failure—natural causes, they said. We were left searching for answers, hoping someone might emerge with more information about the circumstances surrounding her tragic end.

My mom never truly recovered from the loss of her sister. In the beginning, the weight of her grief was suffocating, a heavy blanket that wrapped around her, stifling any flicker of joy. The day her sister passed felt as if a candle had been snuffed out within her, leaving only a faint glow that struggled to survive. We gently suggested she see a grief counselor or talk to us—her friends—anyone who could help. But she stubbornly insisted she was fine, cloaking herself in a facade of strength.

In response, I became hyper-vigilant, my heart racing with an unshakeable urgency. I found myself dialing her number nearly five times a day, a desperate attempt to keep her anchored to this world. I was painfully aware of how fleeting time could be, and that awareness morphed into a cloying neediness. My calls, once a comfort, became a source of irritation for her. "Maybe ease up a bit?" she would say gently, her voice tinged with a weariness that tugged at my heart. But beneath my concern lay a gnawing fear that I dared not voice—our family had already weathered so much.

Determined to pull her from the depths of despair, I sought a distraction for both of us. That's when I proposed a project: what if she wrote stories about her life? I discovered a company that provided weekly prompts to help people recount their memories. Each week, I would ask her a question, and she would respond with her thoughts. Initially, she hesitated, her reluctance obvious, but gradually she warmed to the idea, her curiosity piqued.

As we plunged deeper into this writing journey, I noticed something remarkable: my mother began to transform. Each question I posed seemed to unearth a treasure trove of memories, long buried beneath her grief. She started to share stories of her childhood—tales of mischief and laughter with her sister and brother before he passed away in a tragic motorcycle accident in his early twenties. With each passing week, I watched her eyes shimmer with life as she revisited those moments of pure joy, stories spilling forth like a river breaking free from a dam. The act of remembering became a salve for her wounded heart, gradually rekindling the vibrant woman she had once been, illuminating the shadows that had held her captive for so long.

During the Christmas holidays, we moved slowly, feeling the absence that loss brings while time seemed to rush past us at warp speed. Before we knew it, another year had slipped by. I embarked on a new journey with a job that invigorated me, and we celebrated Christmas and welcomed the New Year once more. As 2024 dawned, I felt a cautious optimism about the opportunities ahead. I embraced my new role as the Director of Inside Sales at a dynamic technology company, finding joy and challenge in equal measure. Meanwhile, Mom gracefully settled into her retirement, savoring the slower pace. Together, we continued to work on our book, making significant strides, and everything else in life seemed to fall into place.

One Monday morning in February, my mom sent a group text to my sisters and me about the mysterious deaths of Black American women who had traveled to The Gambia.

A travel blogger had mentioned my aunt's untimely passing while in Africa and shared her thoughts on Shawn's death in a video that randomly appeared in my mom's online feed. She watched the video in its entirety and wanted to know what each of us thought. Some time after the video was posted, the blogger was found dead. We didn't know what to make of it. So, I emailed Conor at the U.S. Embassy in The Gambia and voiced my concerns about the recent suspicious activity.

"Hello Conor,

It has been nearly two years since you assisted me with the passing of my dear Aunt Audrey. It has come to my attention that, since her death, other African American women have mysteriously died while in The Gambia.

Please take a look at this video that my mother, Audrey's sister, stumbled across."

I attached a link to the video, and Conor replied.

"Hi Diandra,

I hope you are well. I saw the video and have come across a couple of similar videos online. The deaths of U.S. citizens living in The Gambia are tragic, but it is important to remember that The Gambia is a poor, underdeveloped country with very limited healthcare infrastructure. The average life expectancy is 62 years, 14 years less than in the United States.

If you want to pursue an investigation into your aunt's death, I recommend contacting a local attorney first. The police are probably not going to be interested in opening an investigation at this point due to a lack of resources. Some attorneys have investigators who work with them. We have a list of attorneys who have worked with foreigners on cases, which I have provided here.

"All the best, Conor".

I communicated his response to my family, and an unsettling silence enveloped us as we struggled to comprehend its implications. We had taken the precaution of hiring a Gambian attorney, hopeful that she would shed light on the mysterious man Shawn was preparing to marry. Unfortunately, our optimism was misplaced; her lack of diligence rendered our investment in her services futile. Frustrated, we eventually severed ties with her and abandoned our investigation, left with more questions than answers.

The embassy had shipped a few of Shawn's belongings back to my mother, but the heavy air of grief made it impossible for her to find the strength to open the boxes. Each unopened parcel felt like a burial of memories, a refusal to confront the palpable loss that weighed on our hearts. It was a bittersweet moment that marked our reluctant surrender in the face of overwhelming despair.

Tragically, she had died in a manner hauntingly similar to how their mother had passed away. My grandmother, Ruth, had been a vibrant presence in our lives, only 48 years old at her untimely death. She, too, was discovered in a serene state, peacefully asleep, a victim of what the hospital diagnosed as a stroke. The similarities were chilling—a cruel twist of fate that only deepened our sense of loss.

The only solace in the shadow of their departures was the knowledge that both had left this world without suffering, a quiet exit that spared them the pain of anguish. I had to find a way to be at peace with that reality, especially as we stood at a stalemate in uncovering the truth behind Shawn's death. Now, whenever I think of her, I picture her walking along the sun-soaked beach, the wind dancing through her hair, an ethereal vision of beauty. She remains beautiful, forever captured in my memory—a radiant light that will never fade.

CHAPTER 2

WHEN THE RED BIRD APPEARS

A year later, life was gradually returning to normal, each moment stitched together by the passage of time. I found myself immersed in work, traveling extensively to distant cities, where bustling airports and vibrant landscapes became my second home. Meanwhile, my sisters and brother navigated their own journeys, busy with careers, families, and the everyday intricacies of life. The weight of Shawn's death, once an overwhelming shadow that loomed over us, had finally begun to lighten. We had come to a reluctant acceptance, allowing ourselves to breathe again. My mother often reminded us that life ebbs and flows in cycles; for every life extinguished, something new emerges—whether it be strength, resilience, or simply the stubborn will to carry on.

Death had always been a specter of fear in my life. Before Shawn's tragic departure, I had never truly faced the loss of someone dear to me. Yes, my grandfather had passed away nearly a year before Shawn embarked on her pilgrimage to Africa, a departure marked by sorrow yet softened by the understanding that he had lived a full and vibrant life, slowly worn down by Parkinson's disease after a long, arduous battle.

Now, as I reflected on the painful journey we had traversed, I felt a flicker of hope. Mom's cherished project—

a book filled with treasured memories—was nearing completion; we were just three questions away from finishing. Excitement bubbled within me, shared by my mom, as we envisioned the final product encapsulating our family's legacy. We recently gathered to celebrate Mom's 70th birthday with a warm family lunch in Round Rock. It was a day adorned with laughter and love, yet I sensed an underlying tension in her aura.

Although her smile illuminated the room, it felt tinged with something deeper—an unshakeable hesitation to fully embrace her happiness. She voiced a thought fraught with melancholy: "Why am I still here at 70 when my sister never even made it to 55?" In that moment, I understood the heaviness of her survivor's guilt. She wrestled with haunting questions about fate and fairness. What had she done "right" to continue thriving while those she loved had been taken too soon?

No matter how much I wished to alleviate her burden, I knew I couldn't erase the guilt woven into her heart. All I could do was hold her close and remind her that her presence was vital to us. We needed her—our guiding star in a world that often felt too vast and uncertain.

I was sequestered in a dimly lit conference room on a radiant Wednesday afternoon, the sun casting long shadows as it dipped lazily toward the horizon. When I finally returned to my office, the atmosphere felt heavy with impending dread. I glanced at my phone and saw a slew of missed calls and frantic text messages from my twin sister. Urgency gnawed at my insides as I dialed her number.

As soon as she answered, her voice was laced with worry. "Have you talked to Mom today?" she asked. I shook my head, realizing I hadn't heard from our mother since her morning text assuring us she was feeling better. Just days ago, Mom had been uncharacteristically weary, ruminating about ailments she believed were linked to her sinuses. On Tuesday, she had visited the doctor, who administered an IV drip to combat her dehydration, sending her home with instructions to rest and a prescription to help her heal.

Despite her reassurances, my sister and I were troubled by the fatigue etched into her features. The weight of exhaustion had been pulling her down for too long. That morning text had brought a glimmer of hope, a reassurance that she had finally found sleep after a restless night.

As I spoke to my sister, a harrowing panic set in, tightening around my chest like a vice. We constantly urged Mom to answer her phone, often chalking her silence up to her habitual neglect of it. I implored my sister to rush over for a wellness check. We had found ourselves in this worrying situation before, but each time felt like a new shadow creeping closer to our doorstep.

My sister Ylencia was a stone's throw away and sped toward our mother's house, desperation propelling her forward. She rang the doorbell repeatedly, her anxiety mounting as she realized getting in wouldn't be as simple as it seemed—the glass storm door was locked tight. Even though Mom's car was parked protectively in the garage, a knot tightened in my stomach. Finally, after what felt like an eternity, my sister found the elusive key and burst inside. I remained on the phone, my heart racing with fear.

She sprinted to our mother's bedroom, her footsteps echoing in the silence, and then, in an instant that shattered my world, she found her. There lay Mom, vulnerable and still, unclothed and without a breath. Those words, excruciatingly fragile, traveled through the line: "I called 911," she gasped, and a cold wave of dread washed over me. I relayed the details to the operator in Austin, who promptly connected me to the 911 team in Killeen. Urgency elevated my voice as I described the scene. Then, the line clicked dead. I turned back to my sister, only to find she had hung up amidst the chaos. My heart thundered in my ears—it felt as though it had leapt into my throat.

Calming the storm within her, my sister, an occupational therapist, sprang into action. A fierce resolve ignited her movements. She gently covered our mother, lying in a state of stillness, and began administering CPR. Her voice pierced through my panic: "She has no pulse! She has no pulse!" My own breath hitched, adrenaline surging as I screamed—a sound that echoed around me, unnoticed by my colleagues outside my office. My boss appeared suddenly, her presence grounding my spiraling thoughts, and she guided me out of the building with urgency.

Outside, the daylight felt too bright for my swirling emotions. When I finally managed to speak with my sister again, a fragile hope flickered within me. "I heard Mom talking," she reassured me, and I grasped at that thread of light—she would be okay. But just as quickly, that light dimmed as my sister's next words cut through the fragile veil of hope: "I'm sorry, that was Ylencia talking. She's gone... Mom's gone."

The phone slipped from my fingers as we pulled up to my house, numbness washing over me. Ben, my husband, was waiting outside, concern etched on his face. He enveloped me in a comforting embrace, whispering, "Sweets, I'm so sorry. This can't be real." His words echoed my own disbelief. I felt my body crumple like a fragile piece of paper in his grasp. This was not a reality I had ever dared to imagine—a world stripped of my mother's presence.

I struggled to cry, the tears refusing to flow; grief was a weight I couldn't bear to lift. Ben and I stood on the front porch, swaying gently back and forth, two lost souls fighting the impending storm of despair. My boss left quietly, having paid her respects, while I quickly changed my shoes, preparing for the journey north to Killeen. My heart was heavy as I readied myself to face the grief with my sisters and brother.

When we pulled up to Mom's house, there were police investigators outside. My brother was leaning against his car, crying. I dashed out of the car and went to him. We embraced, and he kept muttering, "Mom's gone." We stood like that for a few seconds before I approached the house. My older sister, Ylencia, came out to greet Ben and me. She looked like she had been run over by a Mack truck.

Inside the house, the investigator began to talk to us. He suspected no foul play. She had just... died. We requested an autopsy, and the medical investigators were on their way to take her body for forensics. They announced that they would be wheeling Mom's body into the living room to take her to Dallas for the autopsy. I braced myself as her body entered the room. They said we couldn't touch her. I simply said, "Bye, Mom. I love you." And that was that.

Shortly after, Eddie, our dad, arrived. He had just missed the coroner and forensics team.

"Terry, Ylencia, Dionne, Diandra," he said, almost as if taking roll call. "This is fucked up. I don't know what to say." None of us did. Our relationship with him was, at best, strained. Things had gone awry after he divorced my mom more than 20 years earlier. But it wasn't just a divorce—he had cheated on her with the woman who would later become his new wife. There was no love lost between the two of them, and naturally, we had all sided with Mom.

I still longed for the relationship I once had with my dad. He had been my favorite person growing up, and the irony of him trying to console us about Mom's death, especially after he had all but thrown her away, wasn't lost on me. If this hadn't been so tragic, I might have laughed. Out loud. In his face.

The investigator told us he had found all of Mom's papers. She had thoroughly outlined her last will and testament, leaving information for all her accounts, complete with passwords and logins. She had prepared for her homegoing, even though we weren't ready for it.

The investigator's revelation about Mom's meticulous planning struck a chord. She had faced her mortality head-on, preparing for a future we weren't ready to accept. It was a testament to her strength and foresight—her final gift to us.

As I stood in the living room, surrounded by my siblings, Eddie, and the somber reality of our loss, a profound sense of disbelief washed over me. The chaos of that afternoon—the missed calls, Ylencia's frantic rush, the police, and investigators—all felt surreal, as if I were watching a tragic film unfold rather than living it.

Our father's presence, awkward and strained, added a layer of complexity to our grief. As he struggled for words, I felt a mix of anger and longing. I wanted to remember the man who had once been my hero, but I was coming up empty.

We decided as a group that we wanted to hold the service for her sooner rather than later. We notified her sisters and began the work of organizing her memorial. A few days after her passing, we met with a funeral home and honored her wishes of being cremated. She had never wanted to be buried in the ground. The thought of being placed in a coffin, covered by the earth, was not my mom's idea of resting in eternal peace. In fact, it was her biggest nightmare. She wanted to be cremated, with her ashes divided among her children, and we respected that. I picked out the urn, and we scheduled the memorial service for two weeks later.

But there was the issue of whether Eddie's wife should attend. My brother, sisters, and I had to have an uncomfortable conversation with Eddie because we did not want her there. My dad had cheated on my mom with this woman while he was working overseas in Saudi Arabia after retiring from the military. It was a sordid affair, one my mother had always suspected.

I remember the day she confided in me. I was home from school for the summer, and I noticed she seemed unsettled, like something was bothering her. I had come into the house through the garage, where Eddie was working on my car. The day before, I had answered a long-distance call from a woman who asked for him by name. No one besides my siblings and I ever called him "Eddie." To most, he was either "Ford" or "Sergeant Ford." The call immediately felt wrong, and I remember my stomach doing somersaults as I told the woman, "No, he is not home." I then asked who was speaking, and she hung up.

I marched to the garage, turned down the music my dad was playing, and boldly asked, "Are you cheating on Mom?" He looked at me with wide eyes, lowered them, and scoffed. "Girl, what are you talking about?" I knew instantly that he was lying. I told him the woman had an accent and had specifically asked for him by name. Again, he denied it, telling me I was crazy. That was the moment I lost all respect for my father. I had asked a pointed question as a 21-year-old adult with a strong sense of intuition, and he lied to my face.

That night, I was lying in my parents' bed with my mom when she began talking. Eddie wasn't home—he had gone to Fort Hood to visit the Commissary—so it was just me and her.

"I think Eddie is cheating on me," she said, pulling out his luggage. Inside was a package of condoms. Eddie had had a vasectomy years ago after Dionne and I were born, so why did he need condoms while abroad if he wasn't cheating? I told my mom I was suspicious too and shared the jarring long-distance phone call from earlier. I asked her what she planned to do, and she simply said, "Nothing. He'll come to me when he's ready to stop lying."

We never spoke of it again, but the weight of my mother's words lingered like a shadow over my heart. In a hushed tone, she had implored me to keep the news from my siblings, so I cloaked myself in secrecy, returning to school with a heavy heart that felt as though it were encased in stone. Day by day, I immersed myself in the routine of classes and assignments, yet the knowledge gnawed at me, a persistent reminder of the storm brewing beneath the surface of our family.

Nearly three months had passed since my mother had bared her soul to me when, out of the blue, a call from Ylencia shattered the fragile calm. Her voice crackled through the line, brimming with indignation as she revealed that Mom and Eddie were getting a divorce. "I can't believe you knew about this," she exclaimed, her frustration evident.

The story unfolded like a tragic play: Eddie had ambushed Mom one afternoon while she was engrossed in her lesson plans, papers spread out like a battlefield. With chilling nonchalance, he declared he wanted a divorce. Mom's response was equally cold and cutting—"You can keep the house"—delivered without so much as a glance in his direction. It was a moment of fierce resolve, a testament to her strength in the face of his betrayal.

Memories of how he mistreated and disrespected her flooded my mind, reminders of the deep scars he had inflicted on her spirit. As plans for her memorial began to take shape, those memories ignited a fierce protective instinct within me. There was no way in hell I would allow Eddie to dishonor her legacy. The woman he had cheated on her with—his new wife—was not welcome to parade around her memorial as if the past had evaporated into thin air. My mother would have loathed the thought of her presence, and I was certain she wouldn't have wanted Eddie there either. He was lucky enough to even be allowed to attend.

Just days before the memorial, Eddie had visited Terry for a haircut, brazenly bringing his new wife along. During that visit, she had the audacity to ask Terry what she should wear to the service as if preparing for a social event rather than a somber farewell. Terry, taken aback, immediately reached out to us, his voice trembling with disbelief.

My sisters and I shared a collective sentiment: there was no way she would be allowed to tarnish our mother's memory. We unanimously decided that Terry would be the one to break the news to Eddie. That night, he called and delivered our message clearly: "We don't want her there."

Eddie's response was simple, incredulous: "You all feel this way?" Terry affirmed, hoping that would be the end of it. We breathed a sigh of relief, a brief reprieve from the tension.

But then my phone rang, shattering the moment of calm. It was Eddie, his voice laced with confusion and frustration, asking why his wife could not attend the memorial. The confrontation loomed, and I braced myself for the fallout.

My heart racing, I said, "Eddie, you know damn well why she is not invited. You cheated with this woman, and Mom never forgot it. She may have forgiven you out of the goodness of her heart, but that doesn't give her the right to attend my mother's memorial." He doubled down.

"Well, I'm telling you now. If my wife isn't allowed to attend, then I won't be either," he said with all the arrogance of a narcissistic, philandering man. Without batting an eyelash or even taking a breath, I replied, "So be it. Do what you have to do, but mark my words—I will consider myself fatherless if you don't do right by your kids and your ex-wife." I didn't wait for a rebuttal; I hung up. My siblings and I jumped on a conference call, and I recounted the details of the conversation. They were livid, and Terry proclaimed he would never speak to Eddie again if he stayed true to his word.

As we plunged into the solemn preparations for the memorial, an unexpected surge of confidence compelled me to volunteer to deliver the eulogy. Deep down, I sensed that my mother would have wanted me to do it—her spirit urging me onward. Thankfully, my job granted me the precious gift of time, allowing me to mourn while we meticulously arranged every detail of the service and the subsequent repast.

We chose a charming local hotel for the gathering. Its event space exuded warmth and comfort, while the funeral home provided a serene venue for the memorial service, adorned with soft lighting and delicate floral arrangements. It was beautiful—a fitting tribute to a remarkable woman.

Eddie arrived, impeccably dressed in a dark blue suit and tie, his presence a welcome comfort amid the emotional whirlwind. He came alone, and a wave of relief washed over me as I spotted him seated on the other side of the aisle, his supportive demeanor grounding me in that moment. Beside him were his brother, Emmitt, along with his wife and daughter, their presence a reminder of the community that surrounded us.

As the service unfolded, we shared a poignant video montage—a carefully curated collection of photographs showcasing my mother's vibrant life, accompanied by her favorite song, "Colors" by the Black Pumas. The images flickered on the screen, each one brimming with memories, love, and laughter.

One of the school administrators, a colleague of Mom's, took to the podium to speak eloquently about her profound impact and the innovative Ford Method she had developed. This teaching strategy had not only propelled her students to exceptional scores on the senior aptitude test for English but had also been embraced by the school itself, benefiting countless others. The results were nothing short of remarkable, a testament to Mom's unwavering dedication to education.

Her legacy was one of compassion and excellence. She believed every student deserved the chance to shine, not just those fortunate enough to be in her classroom. As I listened to the heartfelt tributes, I felt an overwhelming swell of pride for the indelible mark she left on so many lives—a legacy that would echo through the corridors of the school and the hearts of her students for generations to come.

When I rose to give the eulogy, I was surprised by the calm and composure I felt. I knew it was important to make my mom proud. As I faced the audience, I began the speech I had carefully prepared. My voice was steady, free from quivers or doubt. She was with me in that moment, guiding me, ensuring that I wouldn't falter.

"Good afternoon. My mother loved the song you just heard in the video tribute; it's called 'Colors' by the Black Pumas. So, let the words resonate:

It's a good day to be, a good day to see

Her favorite colors.

My sisters and my brothers,

We are thankful for the life of our mother

And that you are all here today to celebrate a life well-lived.

I started writing these words about my mom just days ago, and I was going in a much different direction until my sister Ylencia stopped me in my tracks. She advised me to look deep within and really think about capturing the essence and joy that was our mother. She was truly joyful and loved her life. She left the life she had grown accustomed to in her family home to travel overseas with two children under the age of four as a young military spouse. Yes, she was fearful, but she knew this was something she could conquer. This journey was the first of many she would take, and she always made a home for her growing family, wherever we were in the world."

She grew into an adventurous spirit, traveling through Europe with her friends and seeing sights she never imagined as a young girl growing up in Albany, Georgia. She visited Berlin, Holland, and Paris and went on the various field trips that each of us kids had the privilege to experience. She lived to make everything around us beautiful, turning every house we lived in into a home.

Now, all that aside—if you knew my mother well, you know she was a fan of using the entire English language, which did include some choice words. She was never short on words and could hurt your feelings with her honesty, cursing you out with the best of them. She spoke with conviction and meant every word. She would always say, "Raymond Lee was my granddaddy," and he was certainly known for his colorful language—just like her.

And boy, was she funny. Without even trying, she could make you laugh. I can think of countless times we sat around laughing about nothing, just being in her presence was enough to make us feel warm and comforted. My siblings and I have endless "mom-isms"—things only she would say—that we can look back on and smile, even giggle about. There is no shortage of memories that will wrap us in warmth, and for that, we are forever grateful.

She had many passions, but her foremost was being an educator. My mom came from a long line of teachers and dedicated her life to sharing her love of literature with younger generations. Many would say she was a tough teacher, and when students saw their name assigned to her class, there were tears and sighs of grief. But in the end, those students were better for it. Many of her former students and their parents thanked her for her strict teaching style, and she was delighted each time she received such thank-yous and affirmations. It made her happy. It made her feel that, in some small way, she was making an impact—a responsibility she took very seriously.

I thought about my mom's favorite poem, *The Road Not Taken* by Robert Frost. I never fully understood why she loved it so much or why she loved teaching it until I began to dissect it as she would with her students. In the poem, the speaker stands in the woods, considering a fork in the road. Both paths are equally worn and overlaid with undisturbed leaves. The speaker chooses one, telling himself that he will take the other another day, recreating events to say he traveled the road less-traveled.

One would assume that the road in the poem is a metaphor for life, suggesting that we must all choose between two paths—the easier one vs. the harder one, the good one vs. the bad. But Mom would say, "Dig a little deeper." That's too easy, too surface-level. What was Robert Frost really attempting to convey here?

I got frustrated, as I'm sure many of her students did in her class, but I dug deeper. I channeled my inner Sandra Ford, teacher extraordinaire, and realized that the poem is infused with irony. Its title is not *The Road Less Traveled*, but *The Road Not Taken*. Even as the speaker makes a choice, he knows he will second-guess himself somewhere along his journey. What he fails to realize is that there is no *right* path—just the chosen path and whatever option B is.

It's not about making the wrong decision, but about the moments leading up to whatever decision you make. These are the moments that define life. We will endlessly question ourselves. We will feel lost at times, but we must stay the course. This poem doesn't offer advice or tell us where to go or what to do. Instead, Frost's message is more complex. There is no "less-traveled road" in this poem, although the speaker wishes there was. The poem centers on what each individual must do when faced with a "this or that" scenario. Ultimately, Robert Frost is saying, "The choice is yours." It's up to us to choose wisely—if we choose at all.

Mom never told us what to do. Instead, she would always frame her guidance with a question: "What does your heart tell you to do?" or she'd say, "Go with your first mind, child." And that used to frustrate me so much.

I wanted her to tell me what to do, but she never would. She knew that the bulk of her job as a mom was simply to point us in the right direction, let us make the mistakes we were meant to make, and be there to help us pick up the pieces. She was never preachy, always offering a listening ear. I could tell my mother anything without fear of judgment or regret. She was just that caring and loving. She was truly her children's best friend.

She would feign annoyance at my constant calls, but my brother and sisters would say she wasn't kidding—that I was annoying. Still, I just wanted her to know everything about my life. I wanted her involved in every part of it. The void her absence leaves in my life is truly palpable. I am forever changed by her passing, but I am grateful that I got to call her my mom. Mom, you are in a class all by yourself.

I will leave you all with this desideratum: "Go placidly amid the noise and haste, and remember what peace there may be in silence." We will love you always, Mom.

After the heartfelt service, we all made our way to the event space, eager to share a catered meal that would warm our spirits and celebrate the day. In preparation, I had found a lovely event rental company and carefully selected elegant tablecloths, shimmering table runners, and ornate plate chargers that transformed the venue into a welcoming haven. We chose her favorite colors: a luxurious cerulean blue, reminiscent of a clear summer sky, paired with a soft, elegant gray that added a touch of serenity.

As I reflect on that day, I still find it hard to believe how beautifully everything came together, as if love and remembrance wove through each detail. I could almost feel my mom's presence, looking down with pride at her children, who had rallied together to create the most heartfelt homegoing celebration possible, especially given the shock of her sudden passing. A profound longing tugged at my heart as I wished I could ask her what she thought of our efforts. Did we truly make her proud? Was she at peace in a better place?

One tranquil night, as I sat outside on my wraparound porch that hugged the old cedar tree at the edge of the yard, I pondered these thoughts. The air was humid and thick, filled with the soft rustle of leaves and the distant serenade of crickets. I listened intently to the wind chimes she had gifted me, their delicate notes dancing through the night like laughter carried on the breeze. They sounded so light and bright, reminiscent of my mother's joyful spirit.

She had given me the chimes the Christmas before she passed away, her eyes twinkling as she explained that she wanted to leave me something tangible to remind me of her love. I often reflect on that moment, a bittersweet memory filled with longing. Did she have an inkling that her time was near? Did she sense the divine call drawing her toward God and the promise of Heaven?

I've read that when the end approaches, there's an instinctive awareness, a quiet knowing that one's journey is nearing its close. Perhaps that's why she chose to give me the wind chimes in that seemingly random moment—she understood I would need something to bring me comfort in the days to come.

I cherish those wind chimes deeply. Each time I step out of my front door and hear them sound without cause, I pause to whisper, "Hi, Mom," before carrying on with my day. Whether I'm checking the mail or taking the dogs out for a stroll, the sound wraps around me like a warm hug, reminding me of her presence. I feel immensely blessed, grateful for her foresight in giving me this precious token—something that keeps her memory alive and close to my heart.

The day she died, I called a few close friends to tell them of her passing when I got home—only four people. The next day, I received a package from Amazon with a beautiful shadow box inside. It read:

"When tomorrow starts without me,

And I'm not here to see.

If the sun should rise and find your eyes,

Filled with tears for me.

I know how much you love me,

As much as I love you.

And each time you think of me,

I know you'll miss me too.

So when tomorrow starts without me,

Don't think we're far apart.

For every time you think of me,

I'm right here, in your heart."

None of the four people I told had sent this gift, as I asked each one. All the card said was:

"There is nothing I can say to make things better. But I wanted to tell you that you have so many family and friends here for you. I hope this reminds you how much she loved you and how much we love you.

From

— A Friend."

This was indeed very puzzling. The day after she passed away, I received an exquisite shadow box that has held an air of mystery ever since; to this day, I have no idea who sent it. I like to believe it was my mother who orchestrated this heartfelt gift because she understood the tidal wave of grief I would face in the wake of her departure. She had always been so incredibly thoughtful that the notion doesn't seem far-fetched at all. Every time I cast a glance at that shadow box, a gentle smile blooms on my face. And when I hear the enchanting chime of the wind chimes on my porch, I can't help but grin. In those moments, I truly feel her presence enveloping me, as if she were standing beside me, praying for my strength and wishing me peace. In my heart, I know no one could ever take her place—she is irreplaceable, forever etched in my soul.

As I navigated through my days, I began to notice a beautiful phenomenon: cardinals appearing everywhere, almost always in pairs. Their vibrant, ruby-red feathers stood out like little flames against the backdrop of the azure sky, stirring memories of my grandfather's funeral. After the service, we gathered at his home, sharing cherished stories and precious memories, when suddenly, two magnificent cardinals graced the front lawn with their presence. Shawn, ever the comforting soul, remarked that they represented our grandmother and great-grandmother, watching over us during this time of grief. It felt like a warm embrace from the past, a gentle reminder that our loved ones were still with us in spirit, offering solace and love in our moments of sorrow.

There's an old saying that when red birds appear, angels are near. It resonated deeply with me. On the day we received the heartbreaking news of Shawn's death, I was out walking my dogs when three red birds flitted across my path. Their sudden appearance felt like a cosmic affirmation that their spirits would always linger nearby. I embraced the red bird as a gentle nudge from the universe, assuring me that my dearly departed loved ones would always be with me.

I soon found myself captivated by the search for these beautiful creatures, eagerly scanning my surroundings in hopes of catching a glimpse. But as time passed, I learned a vital lesson: you cannot will these moments into existence. You must simply wait for them to cross your path. When you actively seek a blessing, you are sure to overlook it. Now, every time a red bird flutters by or lands gracefully in front of me, it takes my breath away. I can't help but smile, feeling a connection to Mom and Shawn, knowing they would want me to keep moving, filled with hope and love.

CHAPTER 3

LIFE AFTER DEATH

About a month after my mother's passing, Ben and I embarked on a five-day trip to Puerto Rico. We had planned this getaway months in advance, long before the earth-shattering events that had unfolded, and we decided to honor our commitment to this trip. Normally, I would have made it a point to share every detail of our travels with my mother—where we would be staying, how long we would be gone. This time, however, I sent the itinerary to all my siblings, a strange ritual that felt both necessary and unsettling.

As Ben and I wandered through the vibrant streets of San Juan, indulging in the rich flavors of local cuisine and soaking in the sun-drenched beauty of the island, we did our best to enjoy ourselves. We even took a tour of the Bacardi factory and delighted in the rum-infused atmosphere. It was during this carefree moment, cocktail in hand, that my twin, Dionne, called, her voice cracking with urgency. I was savoring my second strong Bacardi drink when I braced myself for the unexpected news she was about to share.

"Guess where I am?" Dionne asked, an edge of excitement in her tone.

"Where?" I replied, my mind racing.

"I'm at the hospital—your niece is in labor."

My heart skipped a beat. My niece, Jadyn, was only 24, just two years out of college and embarking on her career in Adolescent Behavioral Psychology. She didn't even look pregnant; she had recently visited the doctor twice, only to hear the absence of a fetal heartbeat. Yet here she was, unexpectedly in labor. Dionne had taken her to the emergency room, where they discovered she was already a few centimeters dilated. There was no doubt about it—she was having a baby that very day.

The timing was almost surreal. Just one month to the day after my mother's death, a new life was about to enter the world. Edyn Kaye, which was my mother's middle name, made her grand entrance at 12:31 PM on March 21, 2024. In that moment, it felt as though my mother had returned, embodying the joy and warmth we so desperately needed in our time of grief. It was a blessing that felt like a gentle reminder from her spirit, reassuring us that happiness could still flourish amidst sorrow.

Upon returning from Puerto Rico, I made my way to Harker Heights, Texas, eager to meet my grand-niece, Edyn. As I held her in my arms, I marveled at her perfection. It was uncanny how she seemed to inherit some of my mother's cherished mannerisms. I watched as she became mesmerized by her tiny hands, just as my mother had often done. My mom would grip her hands and fiddle with them when lost in thought or overcome with worry; it was a soothing gesture that brought her comfort. Edyn mirrored this habit effortlessly.

Was Edyn, my mother, reincarnated? I've always believed in the afterlife, in the idea that we choose how we return. The irony of Mom selecting Jadyn as her vessel for this new life struck me to my core. Mom and Jadyn shared an unshakeable bond, partners in crime throughout their lives. I like to think that Mom recognized our shared heartache and chose to return, bringing a glimmer of hope to our family in the wake of her absence. A month to the day.

To understand that everything on this earth is meant to be takes a belief in God that is unparalleled. I cannot imagine going through this loss without having any faith. God is awesome, and He does not give you more than you can handle. We embraced Edyn for dear life. A piece of her is my mom, as my mom was hers. She is a beautiful being, and looking at her face is like looking at my mom's. She's so happy and full of life, just as my mom was. Edyn was easygoing and pleasant that it almost took away the void my mom's death left. It was like the adage, "When the replacement from God arrives, you will forget what you've lost."

Edyn's radiant spirit enveloped us, casting a temporary veil over the aching absence of our mother. In her presence, we found a refreshing reprieve, an invigorating breath of fresh air that we had all been longing for, as if we were adrift in a sea of sorrow, gasping for life. Every ounce of love within us was poured into that tiny being, our collective joy manifesting in a way that felt almost sacred. We never questioned the serendipity of her arrival; instead, we embraced it with hearts wide open, grateful for the light she brought into our lives.

Jadyn slipped into her new role as a mother with astonishing grace, embodying an unwavering patience that seemed to calm any storm. I had never envisioned her as a mother—not this soon, at least—but she embraced the challenge fearlessly, effortlessly rising to the occasion. Watching her navigate this new world filled me with admiration; it was as if she had been destined for this path all along.

Before long, we began to settle into our newfound reality, establishing a rhythm that was both comforting and surreal. Ylencia, fully mindful of her responsibilities as the executor of our mother's estate, tackled the meticulous task of organizing Mom's affairs with careful diligence. She took her time, ensuring that every detail was attended to with the utmost respect for our mother's legacy. In the end, we agreed to keep Mom's beloved home, a decision steeped in both practicality and sentiment. Dionne and her husband, Keith, would take up residence there, shouldering the responsibilities that accompanied the cherished space.

Though selling it would have been the easier path, Dionne passionately argued that Mom had poured her heart and soul into that house—she had labored tirelessly to make it a reality, especially after her divorce from Eddie. The house represented more than just bricks and mortar; it symbolized the freedom she had fought to claim, an emblem of her resilience and independence. To her, purchasing that home was a powerful declaration: she no longer needed anyone else to carve out her destiny. It was poetic, really, a testament to her unwavering strength and spirit. She was the guiding light in my life—the woman I idolized. The person I have become is undeniably shaped by her love, the legacy she built, and the invaluable lessons she imparted to us all.

Reaching a decision about my mom's house was anything but simple. The atmosphere was thick with tension as Terry, Ylencia, and I expressed a desire to sell the property and close that chapter of our lives, eager to move on from the bittersweet memories. However, Dionne stood resolutely in her conviction to keep the house in the family, a sanctuary of our shared history and laughter. After intense discussions that felt like an emotional tug-of-war, we finally brokered a compromise:

Dionne and her husband, Keith, would move in later that summer, ensuring that our mother's cherished home remained filled with love.

Mom had always been impeccably organized, so when it came time to sort through her affairs, we were met with a treasure of meticulously kept records—everything from banking information to mortgage papers laid out with precision. Ylencia, shouldering the burden of responsibility, was tasked with notifying various companies of our mother's passing. I admired her resilience; I certainly didn't envy the significant work ahead of her on behalf of our mom. Yet, despite the weight of the task, Ylencia rose to the occasion, honoring our mother's wishes with unwavering determination.

Throughout this process, Dionne and Terry clashed repeatedly, their disagreements echoing through the house like a storm. Yet, amid the chaos, we reminded ourselves of our mother's legacy—her unwavering belief that we should stand together as a united front. She had instilled in all of us the values of perseverance, strength, and the importance of living life fully. Mom's heart swelled with joy when her children were happy and united. In her presence, love and harmony flourished, even amidst the family's often tumultuous dynamics.

I felt a profound responsibility to maintain the strong bonds I had cultivated with my siblings, honoring her memory and teachings. Reflecting on our journey, I believe we all managed to uphold those relationships, carrying forward the spirit of togetherness that Mom cherished so dearly. Together, we honored her memory and our shared past, forging a path toward healing and unity.

CHAPTER 4

THE INTERIM

In the wake of my mother's passing, an oppressive weight settled over my heart, enveloping me in a shroud of despondency. The vibrant colors of my life faded into muted shades of gray, and a month after her departure, I found myself at a crossroads—my soul aching for change. My role as Director of Inside Sales, once a source of pride, had turned into a prison. I could no longer ignore the hollow echoes of discontent resonating deep within me.

One early Wednesday morning, as the sun began to cast soft rays through my window, I dialed my boss's number with trembling hands. My heart raced, a tempest of emotions swirling inside me as I uttered the words that would alter the course of my life: "Today will be my last day." In my 22-year sales career, I had never done such a thing. I had always been an advocate for the two-week notice, a loyal employee. But in that moment, the chains of obligation shattered. I felt an urgent need to prioritize my mental well-being. A flicker of defiance ignited within me as I recognized that this relentless grind was not where I was meant to be.

I turned my back on the security of a paycheck that had once seemed paramount, realizing that the substantial pay cut I had accepted no longer resonated with my spirit. I could hear my mother's voice, warm and insistent, nudging me gently: "Go with your first mind, child." And so, I acted swiftly and decisively, unburdened by doubt or second-guessing. For the first time in what felt like forever, I chose to prioritize my happiness over the expectations of others.

With every step away from that office, I felt a sense of liberation—a weight lifting off my shoulders. I no longer wanted to remain in a space that didn't value my talents, that diminished my worth, that made me feel small in a world where I longed to be cherished. Being unemployed granted me the precious gift of time—time to reflect, grieve, and finally confront the avalanche of emotions I had buried deep in the aftermath of my mother's death.

In the chaotic weeks following her passing, I had been on autopilot—moving through life as if I were merely a spectator, suppressing the profound sorrow clawing at my insides. My mother had been a colossal presence in my life, and the ache of her absence was insurmountable. You don't simply move on from such a loss.

I recalled the five stages of grief: denial, anger, bargaining, depression, acceptance. I had traversed denial and tasted the bitterness of anger, but the heart of my journey—acceptance—remained elusive. At the five-month mark, I hit a wall, plummeting into a deep depression from which it felt impossible to climb out. This emotional turmoil became the catalyst for my impulsive decision to quit my job without a safety net. I had diligently amassed savings and was prepared to take a leap of faith, embracing uncertainty with open arms.

"Sometimes you gotta step out on faith and do the thing that scares you to show you that you must and can trust in God," my mother had always said. I held onto those words as I began to listen—to the voice of Sandra Kaye Ford echoing within me as I embarked on my Boss Bitch Era. Life was far too brief for hesitation and regret.

Her passing illuminated an undeniable truth: life is precious and fleeting, and it is the relentless pursuit of joy, authenticity, and courage that we must cherish above all else.

One evening, as I sat in quiet reflection, my thoughts drifted to my mother's sisters and how they were faring in the wake of her death. Only one of them, my aunt Jaquelyn, had graced the memorial service with her presence. Tanya had chosen to embark on a long-planned cruise, prioritizing her getaway over family, while Patricia seemed indifferent, opting to remain absent despite being just an hour away visiting Jaquelyn. The contrast was stark. Jaquelyn stood before us, her words weaving a tale of memories that celebrated my mother's spirit, and I felt a surge of gratitude that she was there. She had always been one of my closest aunts, a comforting presence in my life, especially during the early days of my sales career at Dell when I had sought her guidance and support.

But Patricia's absence weighed heavily on my heart. She had spun a narrative that suggested we harbored resentment toward her, rooted in a bitter fallout between her and my mother following their father's death. In her mind, attending the service would have been an unwelcome intrusion. I found it unfathomable that someone could turn their back on their own sister's funeral. For me, the thought of missing such a pivotal moment in my siblings' lives was unimaginable.

The rift between my mother and Patricia was deep and painful. My mother believed Patricia had betrayed their father, failing to care for him while pocketing his hard-earned money and masquerading her actions as acts of kindness. The truth was far more sinister. Patricia had siphoned hundreds of thousands of dollars from him, treating his life savings as though they were her due, with no regard for his dignity and health.

It fell to Shawn to step in as the primary caregiver when my grandfather's condition reached a critical low. I vividly recall the winter of 2018 when he visited Texas; it was a miracle he had even made the journey. His frail body, shrunken and weary, bore the weight of neglect. After witnessing his decline, Shawn made a resolute decision. She left her home in North Carolina, moving in with him to provide the care he so desperately needed. With her nurturing touch, she took him to Parkinson's therapy classes, and, to our astonishment, he began to thrive once more. It was a powerful reminder of the transformative effects of love and genuine care.

My grandfather, though far from perfect, deserved so much more than the treatment he received. He had spent his life battling his own shortcomings, striving to make amends for past mistakes, just as we all do in our imperfect human existence. My mother often reminded us of her own fallibility, openly acknowledging the mistakes she made while raising us. Yet it was her ability to recognize those flaws and strive to correct them that made her truly remarkable. In her journey of growth and self-improvement, she embodied the essence of what it means to be human. Isn't the pursuit of becoming the best version of ourselves the ultimate goal in life?

Despite my best efforts, I could never fully grasp the emotional complexity of caring for a family member—especially a father—who had inflicted so much pain throughout your life. My mother and her sisters endured countless trials with their own father, a man whose struggle with alcohol-fueled a tempest of abuse and heartache for them and my grandmother. It takes an extraordinary individual to set aside deep-seated grievances and extend love and compassion, especially when that love feels like a betrayal of one's own suffering. Yet Shawn embraced this challenge with unwavering strength, pouring every ounce of her being into the role of caretaker.

Together, she and my mother formed a formidable team. While Shawn stood by their father's side, assisting him with his daily activities, my mother provided steadfast support from afar, her heart tethered to them despite the miles that separated them. It was a beautiful sight, witnessing their bond flourish in the face of past traumas; their shared purpose as caretakers for their father transcended the bitter memories of their childhood. However, the chasm between my mother, Shawn, and the other sisters deepened irreparably. My mother was adamant that she would never again speak to Patricia, who had so brazenly exploited their father's struggles to benefit herself.

This vow held firm until the day my mother passed away. The conspicuous absence of her sisters at her memorial served as stark validation of her choice. My siblings and I echoed her sentiments, choosing to distance ourselves from the toxicity that had long plagued our family. My mother was nothing if not passionate, fiercely protective of her own feelings and those of the people she loved. While the decision to sever ties was excruciating, she recognized it as necessary for her own peace of mind. How could she maintain a genuine relationship with those who had so shamelessly exploited their father without a hint of remorse or acknowledgment of their wrongdoing? It was unfathomable to her, and I often pondered what I would do if faced with a similar betrayal from one of my siblings— especially knowing that my father, like my grandfather, was far from perfect.

The thought of cutting ties with any of my siblings, with whom I share an unbreakable bond, felt unbearable. I can only imagine the pain my mother endured, and it lingers with me still—the weight of her heart-wrenching decision. Sometimes, choosing yourself means making the hardest of choices, and that was precisely what she did. It is a bitter irony that throughout her life, she had been the epitome of selflessness. I reflect on the countless sacrifices she made, filled with admiration for the strength and resilience she embodied.

CHAPTER 5

IN THE BEGINNING

I grew up a military child, moving every three years as a result. My dad was a scout in the Army, and we lived overseas for most of my youth. I'm so thankful for that experience and the vast world I got to see beyond the U.S. It wasn't until we moved back to the States that I first encountered racism. Moving frequently made starting over and forging relationships easy for me. I loved going to new schools and reinventing myself—it was an adventure I always welcomed. My mom encouraged our adventurous spirits, taking us on field trips to explore all the towns, big and small, throughout Europe. She also went on trips with her friends to places she never dreamed of visiting—Paris, Holland, London. The military afforded her opportunities beyond her wildest dreams. What a blessing that was.

Back in the States, we were living in Georgia between base transfers when we received the news that my dad had to leave to fight in the Gulf War. I was eight years old. Adjusting to life in my parents' hometown of Albany, Georgia, was tough. It was a small town, and we were essentially a displaced military family due to the war, moving from house to house. We were close to an Air Force base, and my mom pleaded with them to let us live on base near Cromartie Beach. In the meantime, we stayed with one of my great aunts, but she eventually kicked us out. We then moved to the "country" where my mom had grown up, staying at my great-grandmother's house. She welcomed us with open arms until we were finally able to move onto the Air Force base.

The joy of moving into our new home was palpable. With each passing day, life settled into a comforting rhythm, slowly returning to something resembling normalcy. Dionne and I were excited to start our new adventure at Dougherty County Middle School, where the hallways buzzed with the chatter and laughter of other students. Meanwhile, my older sister and brother were navigating life at Dougherty County High School, facing their own challenges and triumphs.

Dionne, however, carried a heavier burden. For years, she had bravely battled the effects of scoliosis, her fragile spine curving like an elegant "S." After countless doctor's visits and hopeful treatments, the specialists finally reached a difficult conclusion: she would need major surgery to correct the dangerous curvature threatening her health. The weight of this decision loomed over us, especially since we were just eleven years old, grappling with fears that seemed far too big for our young hearts.

In the midst of this turmoil, a glimmer of hope arrived when my dad was granted leave from the war to come home. The day he arrived at the regional airport in Albany is etched in my memory—a rush of emotions as we saw him step through the terminal doors, his face lighting up with the warmth of homecoming. The school even held a special ceremony to honor him, where he stood before us as a figure of strength and courage, speaking eloquently about his experiences during the war and the deep ache of being separated from his family for more than two years. In that moment, I felt an overwhelming sense of pride for my dad, recognizing him not just as my father but as a hero who had faced extraordinary challenges with resilience and grace.

Dionne was in recovery from her more than seventeen-hour surgery. She spent weeks in the ICU before being moved to a private room, where she began the slow path to walking again. She had been bedridden for so long that she had to relearn basic motor skills. It was a strange time for me. Dionne and I were as close as could be, and it felt odd that she was unable to do so many things. Learning to walk again and regain strength took a toll on her, but I marveled at how strong she was at such a young age. Eventually, my dad returned to the desert, and we waited another year until the war was finally over. I wrote to him constantly, as I missed him terribly. Terry, my older brother, was now a teenager and spiraling out of control. He was out drinking and partying most weekends.

When we finally left Georgia and PCS'd to Louisiana, Terry decided to finish out his final year of high school in Georgia and didn't come with us.

We were stationed at Fort Polk, nestled in the pines of Leesville, Louisiana—a small town alive with the sounds of chirping cicadas and the rustle of oak leaves in the warm, humid air. After years of embracing the role of a dedicated stay-at-home mom, my mom felt the familiar tug of ambition. She expressed her desire to return to the workforce, and the excitement in our household was palpable. With Ylencia at the vibrant age of fourteen and Dionne and me just eleven, we were blossoming into our independence, ready to support her as she ventured into this new chapter.

When Mom applied for a position at the local library, it felt like the perfect fit—a soothing place filled with the soft rustle of pages and the comforting scent of old books. To our delight, she landed the job, allowing her to maintain a balanced schedule while we adjusted to her new routine. Yet, deep down, Mom craved more. She longed to revisit her passion for teaching high school English, the subject she loved sharing with eager minds. Fueled by determination, she immersed herself in rigorous study for the Louisiana teacher exam. When she finally passed, it felt like a triumphant victory.

With her new role at Leesville High School, Mom officially became a Wampus Cat—the school mascot—bound to inspire students and instill knowledge. For Ylencia, the situation was bittersweet. She found herself navigating the hallways of the same school as our mother, earning a few sympathetic glances from classmates. Dionne and I didn't envy Ylencia's predicament. Mom quickly earned a reputation as a no-nonsense teacher—her classroom was a realm of discipline and focus, where students dared not cross her. But in her eyes, there was a flicker of joy every time she entered that classroom, bringing literature and grammar to life with her passionate lectures and unwavering standards.

After three years at Fort Polk, our journey took us to the expansive landscapes of Fort Hood, Texas. It felt like breathing in a new world, where the skies stretched wider and the sun shone brighter. Dionne and I were stepping into the challenging world of high school as freshmen, filled with a mixture of excitement and trepidation, while Ylencia was reluctantly gearing up for her senior year at Ellison High School alongside us. Meanwhile, Terry, our older brother, continued his path in Georgia, charting his course in life without the pressure of academics hanging over him.

As Ylencia graduated from Ellison and was accepted to Baylor University, a prestigious private institution in Waco just a stone's throw away, the joy in our home was infectious. It marked a thrilling milestone, and she embraced every moment, reveling in the freedom and camaraderie of college life. Mom had seamlessly transitioned to teaching 6th-grade English at Smith Middle School, and Eddie remained proudly dedicated to his service in the Army, each of us carving out our respective paths while cherishing the joyful chaos of family life.

When we graduated high school, I set my sights on Texas State University, then known as Southwest Texas State University. With dreams of breaking into the world of broadcasting—whether crafting captivating articles for *Vogue* or lighting up the screen as an on-air personality—I felt a mix of excitement and trepidation. Eager to immerse myself in the vibrant arts scene, I joined the Black theater troupe, a decision that initially made me feel at home amidst the creative chaos of campus life. Yet beneath that enthusiasm, gnawing homesickness settled in, creeping into my spirit like a relentless shadow.

Over time, that homesickness transformed into a physical manifestation as cruel as it was unexpected. I was diagnosed with an autoimmune disease called Hidradenitis Suppurativa, a condition that wreaked havoc on my body. The way it manifested was utterly awful—a cyst the size of a tennis ball developed in my left armpit, a grotesque reminder of the pain I was enduring.

The first time it appeared, the anguish was unbearable, rendering my arm almost immobile. I remember the distress etched on my mother's face as she drove all the way from Killeen to San Marcos to pick me up. Our drive back to Killeen felt long and suffocating, punctuated by my fearful anticipation of what awaited me at the doctor's office.

Once we arrived, they lanced the cyst that very day, and I was wide awake, grappling with agony that bordered on unbearable, even with pain medication. In the haze of that moment, my thoughts spiraled around the realization that I was on the brink of passing out. The ordeal left me reeling, and I soon faced a difficult choice: taking a leave of absence from school to recuperate while receiving home health care. For six grueling weeks, a nurse came to our home every day, meticulously unpacking and repacking the dressings on my wound. This was perhaps the lowest point of my eighteen years, a time when I yearned—more than anything—for normalcy amidst the storm of constant pain and spontaneous flare-ups.

I could only watch from the sidelines as my friends indulged in the carefree college experience that I so desperately craved. Ylencia, in particular, seemed to embody everything I wanted. She thrived at Baylor, rushing into her senior year with a flamboyant charm, a handsome boyfriend, and the kind of life that glimmered with promise. I couldn't help but feel a simmering resentment toward the universe, but mostly toward my unruly body that seemed to betray me when I needed it most. The flare-ups persisted relentlessly, and by my junior year, managing the disease alongside my studies became unbearable. I found myself failing miserably, wrestling with the harsh reality of dropping out of college, burdened by the weight of disappointment and guilt for wasting my parents' hard-earned money. With my head hung low, I packed up the meager belongings in my single-person dorm room and made the long journey back home.

Determined to occupy my newfound free time, I set out to find a job. Lacking sufficient transferable skills, I accepted a position at Sallie Mae, processing student loans for other college students—an ironic twist, considering I had just walked away from my own academic journey, only a few credits shy of a degree. I spent about a year there before discovering that Dell was hiring contract workers, an opportunity that sparked my desire for a fresh start. This led me to Austin, where I moved in with my Aunt Jaquelyn. For the first time in a long while, I felt a flicker of happiness.

At Dell, I met a remarkable group of people who would become lifelong friends. As I transitioned from living with Jakki to settling into a stylish condo just a few miles from her home and close to work, my life slowly transformed. It was at one of my favorite bars, Agave, where I crossed paths with my now best friend, Payal. We exchanged numbers as if exchanging lifelines, and we quickly became inseparable, spending every weekend reveling in our newfound companionship. My Hidradenitis Suppurativa was in remission, allowing me a taste of normalcy I thought I had lost forever. I was living for the moment, embracing the joy of new friendships and experiences—until, inevitably, that fragile sense of equilibrium began to crumble.

I silently battled my mental health for years, a struggle that reached a breaking point the summer I turned 25. As the days grew warmer, I found myself retreating further into solitude, my once vibrant spirit dimming as responsibilities slipped through my fingers. Bills piled up, reminders of my neglect, while I sank deeper into an overwhelming abyss of depression—though, at that time, I didn't even recognize it for what it was. I believed I was simply failing, a loser unable to rein in the chaotic thoughts that consumed me.

One fateful day, weighed down by despair, I made my way to the pharmacy. With sweaty hands, I purchased a large bottle of sleep medication, my heart heavy with a decision that felt like the only escape. When I returned home, I meticulously tidied my apartment, ensuring it was immaculate—a final act of control amidst the chaos. I sat down to write goodbye letters, pouring my heart into each one, crafting a farewell to every member of my family. As the clock inched toward 7 PM, I pressed play on "End of the Night" by Kenny G, the smooth saxophone melodies echoing through the silence of my home.

With a sense of finality, I dumped the bottle of pills onto the kitchen bar, the white tablets glistening under the light like tiny harbingers of my decision. A sheet of paper lay beside me, a makeshift tally for each pill I swallowed, one by one, until the bottle was empty and my tick sheet was full. In that moment, I was oblivious to the plans I had made with Payal for that very evening. As the darkness began to envelop me, consciousness slipped away, leaving only the haunting notes of the saxophone in the background.

Suddenly, I was jolted back to reality by the sound of hurried footsteps racing up the stairs, accompanied by a familiar voice calling my name. Payal, growing increasingly anxious after receiving no response to her messages, had come to check on me. Using her spare key, she let herself into my apartment, her worry morphing into panic as she realized something was terribly wrong. In a flurry of movement, she dialed 911, her voice trembling as she relayed the urgency of the situation. Moments later, paramedics arrived, swiftly loading me onto a gurney and carrying me away from the sanctuary of my apartment. The bright lights of the hospital loomed ahead—a place that might just hold a flicker of hope amidst the darkness.

I found myself in the stark, fluorescent-lit chaos of the emergency room, a tangle of tubes and IVs snaking from my arm, tethering me to the sterile environment. The medical team bustled around me, their voices a blur as they informed me that Payal had arrived just in the nick of time—before I could inflict irreversible damage to my organs. Desperation clawed at my throat, and I pleaded with them to let me slip away, to simply allow me to die. In response, they presented me with two grim choices: drink a foul concoction of activated charcoal to absorb the pills I had taken, or endure the invasive process of having my stomach pumped. Time was slipping through my fingers like sand, and I realized I had to decide quickly. With a heavy heart, I opted for the charcoal. I don't know why. I guess I just wanted to give myself another chance at life.

As the gritty substance settled in my stomach, a wave of nausea washed over me—an unwelcome reminder of the numerous glasses of water I had consumed in a futile attempt to wash down the pills. I summoned the courage to ask to use the restroom, desperation urging me forward. A nurse kindly assisted me, her gentle touch a comfort as I hurried to relieve myself.

But the moment I stood up from the toilet, everything spiraled out of control. My IV slipped from my arm, and crimson droplets splattered against the sterile tile, painting a stark contrast to the pristine environment. Panic surged through me as I pressed the call button, but the sight of my own blood became too much to bear. Darkness enveloped me, and I collapsed onto the cold floor.

I awoke to an unexpected sensation—a warm, gentle dampness on my forehead. Blinking through the haze, I realized it was my mother, tears streaming down her face as she hovered over me. The anguish reflected in her eyes was a pain I had never wanted to witness. In the waiting room, I could see my aunts, Jaquelyn and Shawn, along with my sisters and their husbands, all waiting with bated breath. That evening, I was moved to the ICU, where the doctors expressed concern over potential damage to my kidneys and liver. For three long days, I remained there, a patient under watchful eyes, until my mom made the heart-wrenching decision to have me committed to a psychiatric hospital. Reluctantly, I accepted her insistence; she could not drop everything to care for me, not while I remained alone in my apartment, a single woman adrift in a sea of despair.

As I was loaded into the back of a Constable's squad car, I cast one last glance at my mom and Payal, their faces etched with worry as we drove away. Fear gripped me tightly; I had nothing with me—no shoes, no lip gloss, no phone—just the weight of uncertainty pressing down on my chest.

Upon arriving at the hospital, a nurse awaited me, ready to lead me inside. Though I cannot recall the exact words the officer spoke, I remember the kindness in his voice—a soothing warmth in my turbulent world. I wish I could have expressed my gratitude more eloquently, but in that moment, all I could muster was a faint nod, overwhelmed by the kindness of a stranger when I felt most lost.

The smell of the psychiatric hospital still clung to my nostrils—a blend of antiseptic and something far more unsettling, an odor of neglect and despair. It was dingy and old, just like the scenes from horror films that flickered in the back of my mind, where darkness loomed in every corner. Dimly lit hallways stretched out before me, and patients shuffled about, their murmurs a haunting soundtrack of disconnection. A wave of confusion washed over me; all I knew was that I wanted to escape this oppressive place.

I had arrived late in the afternoon, the fading light hinting that "lights out" would be soon. A nurse hurried me into a sterile intake room, where I was subjected to a humiliating strip search. Afterward, I was handed a pair of thin socks, a toothbrush, and a tiny tube of toothpaste—my only possessions in this unsettling new reality. The nurse guided me down a long, stark corridor, finally stopping in front of a small room occupied by a frail, white-haired woman who lay sleeping, her chest rising and falling rhythmically. The nurse pointed me toward my bed and flicked off the light, plunging me into darkness.

I climbed into the narrow cot, tears streaming down my cheeks as the coldness of the room seeped into my bones. All I had for warmth was a flimsy sheet and a worn quilt that barely did the job. I don't know how long I lay there, lost in a haze of confusion, but eventually, sleep claimed me. I woke to the news that I would be transferred to a private room the following morning, a flicker of hope igniting within me. If I had to endure this place, I preferred solitude over the chaos of shared quarters.

The next day, as they escorted me to my new room, a loud bell suddenly resonated through the corridors, its alarming clang sending shivers down my spine. I turned to the orderly beside me, anxiety bubbling up inside. "What does that mean?" I asked, my voice barely above a whisper.

She met my gaze with a calm, practiced expression. "It's med time," she replied, her tone devoid of emotion.

As we walked past the great room, I caught sight of a line forming—patients extending their hands toward the nurse's station like supplicants at a temple of treatment. I wanted no part of that ritual. During my intake, I had refused medication, craving clarity in a world that felt utterly muddled. I needed to confront whatever emotions awaited me, raw and unfiltered.

That afternoon, I attended a group therapy session, where the stories of my fellow patients unfolded like the pages of a tragic novel. Listening to their experiences was both enlightening and humbling. Was my life truly so bad? I had a decent job, friends who cared, and a family that loved me. Yet many in the room had been cast aside, living on the streets, estranged from their loved ones. Their circumstances were heartbreaking.

Suddenly, the community phone rang, slicing through the somber atmosphere. Someone called my name. It was my dad on the other end, his voice a welcome comfort. "Ana, do you want me to come get you?" he asked, using the nickname he had called me for as long as I could remember. Tears flowed freely as I realized how much I wanted to leave this place. But my mom, steadfast in her decision, insisted I stay for the two weeks she had committed me to, her authority over my treatment plan a heavy weight I could not escape. I had long forgotten the medical power of attorney I had granted her during my struggles with HS, and now I found myself trapped, unable to have visitors, forced to bide my time.

In the solitude of my confinement, I resolved to take stock of my life and picked up journaling once more. It became my refuge, the only way to fill the hours when I wasn't in group therapy. I began to open up to those around me; nothing humbles you more than a mental breakdown, it seemed.

As I laid everything out on those pages, I slowly pieced together the fragments of my life. I realized that my struggles stemmed from deep-seated issues of self-worth—an ever-present shadow. I had battled with my weight for as long as I could remember, my life a relentless cycle of eating, guilt, and self-loathing. My relationship with my mother was fraught with tension; her critical words, often labeling me as "fat," echoed in my mind, solidifying the body image issues that followed me into adulthood.

Towering at five feet seven inches, I felt out of place among my sisters, who were just a smidge over five feet. I longed to be smaller, to fit the mold of what I thought was desirable. My attempts to shrink myself were pointless. I frequently slouched to take away some of my height, but all that did was give me bad posture. I would binge eat for a day, then not eat anything for the next two or three days. My weight fluctuated frequently, and I was elated each time my pants fit a bit more loosely. But that jubilation quickly turned to self-hate if I gained even a pound. It was impossible to maintain my weight, and I felt trapped inside my own body. The criticism from my mom and the self-inflicted criticism played a huge role in my depression. That is what I finally learned about myself while in the psychiatric facility.

Years later, as the tides of our relationship began to shift toward a fragile reconciliation, my mom would sit across from me, her eyes brimming with unshed tears, and confess her regrets. "I made mistakes with you," she would say, her voice trembling with the weight of unspoken guilt. The pain etched on her face spoke volumes about the turmoil I had endured, and deep down, she held herself accountable. The room would fill with the heavy silence of her remorse as she made her apologies, each one laced with the sorrow of a mother longing to mend broken bonds. All I could do was respond with forgiveness, offering her the grace she had struggled to extend to herself.

We had arrived at a better place together, one built on the foundation of understanding and healing. In my journey toward self-improvement, I began to learn the importance of treating myself with kindness and compassion, giving myself the grace that had so often felt out of reach. My mom, too, was undergoing her own transformation, navigating the rocky path toward becoming her best self. Her apologies served as a catalyst, propelling our relationship forward, as her admission of past wrongs validated the emotions I'd carried for so long. I realized that I hadn't been imagining the neglect and mistreatment of my younger self; it was real, and her acknowledgment of it soothed a deep ache within me.

For years, I'd wrestled with my issues around food, convinced they were little more than figments of my imagination. In truth, her lack of support during my formative years had significantly contributed to my fragile self-esteem, coming at a time when encouragement could have made a monumental difference. The resentment I harbored for her, born from that absence, began to dissipate with her heartfelt apology. I instinctively knew I needed to liberate myself from the weight of food and the obsession with achieving an unattainable thinness. It became imperative for me to embrace love for myself, no matter the shape or size I occupied. However, this was not just a fleeting thought; I understood that I would be grappling with societal pressures, and cycling through fad diets, surgeries, and weight-loss medications for years to come. It was a daily commitment, a steadfast choice I had to make to cultivate a healthier relationship with myself.

After my two-week stay in the psychiatric unit, I was finally allowed to return home. My dad picked me up in the sweltering summer heat, the air heavy with the scent of blooming flowers, and drove me from Austin to my mother's house. She welcomed me with open arms, determined to guide me through the fragility of my recovery. Together, we sought out a psychiatrist to help me navigate the next steps on my healing journey. The process of finding the right psychiatric medication felt daunting; it was a delicate balancing act as we experimented with different options. I tried Lexapro, Bupropion, and several others, each with its own set of side effects that left me feeling adrift. At last, I found a medication that worked wonders with minimal issues—Abilify—bringing a sense of equilibrium back to my life. For the first time in what felt like an eternity, I caught a glimpse of "normal," whatever that meant for me.

Diagnosed with severe depression, I learned the importance of consistency in my medication regimen as I navigated the emotional triggers that awaited me in daily life. I began therapy, attending weekly sessions where I peeled back layers of pain and learned how to rebuild. Feeling a glimmer of hope after months of darkness, I returned to work after three months of leave. My mother had skillfully conversed with my boss, ensuring all the paperwork was in place for my much-needed time off. As I stepped back into the workplace, gratitude washed over me. I was thankful for the job I was going back to, a stepping stone on my continuing journey toward healing and self-acceptance.

Returning to my modest apartment, I felt a mix of gratitude and guilt brewing within me. Mom had selflessly covered my rent throughout my struggle, a gesture so profound that I found myself at a loss for how I could ever repay her. Remarkably, she never once brought up the matter of money; it was as if she intended to erase the debt from my mind entirely, allowing me space to heal without the weight of obligation. As I gradually reacquainted myself with the rhythm of work, I noticed a burgeoning sense of confidence flowering within me, a quiet contentment slowly taking root in my life.

It struck me profoundly how infrequently people engage in conversations about mental health, a topic often wrapped in layers of stigma and shame, particularly within the Black community. In my own life, I had become a regular presence at my therapist's office—an oasis of comfort and understanding—where each session unfolded like a carefully crafted ritual, leading me closer to the liberation I sought. In that warmly lit room, where the air was thick with empathy, I discovered the transformative power of articulating my innermost thoughts and feelings.

Discussing my struggles became a cherished act; I looked forward to these moments of honesty and connection, each one a gentle reminder of the profound healing that comes with embracing vulnerability.

Yet, despite my progress, I found myself ensnared in a web of confusion, questioning the motivations behind my past actions. My mind relentlessly sought understanding, yearning to untangle the intricate threads of my struggles. An urgent need stirred within me—a desire to recognize the subtle warning signs that might indicate a faltering mental state in the future. Thus, I embarked on a journey of self-exploration through daily journaling, pouring the unfiltered contents of my heart onto the pages like a river in flood, each entry a chaotic outpouring of thoughts swirling in a wild dance of emotions.

Interestingly, I noticed a hesitance within myself to fully plunge into the abyss of darkness that had once engulfed me. As I reflected on the past, I traced the roots of my depression back to my high school years, where the battleground of self-worth was fought daily. Throughout those tumultuous teenage years, I wrestled with a persistent sense of inadequacy, an overwhelming impression that I would never embody the societal standard of desirability. My tooth gap, a noticeable and often ridiculed void between my two front teeth, only intensified my self-loathing, fueling the conviction that I was somehow repulsive. This deeply ingrained belief convinced me over the years that no one could ever truly desire me.

The quest for self-love felt like a distant dream, an elusive concept shimmering just beyond my grasp. Yet, it was precisely that essence I craved—an acceptance of myself that lingered just out of reach, beckoning me to pursue it feverishly.

In my youthful naiveté, I had known the intoxicating essence of love only once—a fleeting yet profoundly impactful experience with my first boyfriend, whom I met during the vibrant dawn of adulthood at the tender age of eighteen. He was a soldier stationed at Fort Hood, embodying a sense of adventure and bravery that captivated me completely. In the midst of my otherwise dim and mundane world, he shone brightly, his presence igniting a spark of joy and hope that I had never before encountered. His ambitions, however, soon took him far from the familiar comforts of Texas, as he sought higher education and dreamed of a life that extended beyond the confines of military service.

Our relationship transformed into an intricate dance of separation, marked by long-distance phone calls that bridged the miles between us and heartfelt letters, each carefully penned and filled with our deepest thoughts and emotions. Strangely, the distance brought a peculiar comfort. It spared me from the vulnerabilities and intimate demands of daily commitment, allowing me to savor the sweetness of our connection while still nurturing my own independence. We cherished the few weekends we spent together, where time felt both fleeting and eternal, creating a bubble of joy in the otherwise chaotic world around us.

For three long years, we navigated the challenges of a long-distance relationship, our hearts tethered by a thread of hope. But as life's wheels turned relentlessly, we found ourselves gradually diverging onto different paths, each pursuing our own dreams and aspirations. Now, he is happily married, enveloped in the warmth of a bustling family—an image that feels almost surreal to me, as it's something I could never envision for myself. The thought of children and the responsibilities that come with motherhood felt like an anchor, tethering me down and stifling my ambitions. I yearned to ascend the ranks in my sales career, to chase after my dreams without the weight of familial obligations dulling my pursuit. I was determined to carve out a life full of achievement and fulfillment without surrendering my freedom.

Often, during candid conversations with my mom, I would confide in her about my lack of maternal instinct and my hesitance toward raising children. Her response was always laced with wisdom: "Of course not. If I had to do it all over again, I don't know if I would have chosen children for myself. You're experiencing the adventures I never got to have. Embrace your freedom—love will ebb and flow, but right now, you have your career and your independence. Live fiercely and without regret." Her unflinching honesty resonated deeply within me. She was transparent about her own regrets, yet she never shamed me for being single or for my decision to remain child-free. Instead, her words became a soothing balm, instilling a sense of pride in my choices.

I was fortunate to have a family that embraced an evolved perspective on life—those nagging questions of "When will you settle down?" never tainted our conversations. In many ways, we were trailblazers—strong, independent women, a testament to the formidable influences of our matriarchs.

CHAPTER 6

FINDING HAPPINESS

It had been nearly twelve long years since my dramatic fall from grace, a period marked by difficult lessons and profound transformations. Now, I found myself embracing life with a renewed sense of vitality and exuberance, reveling in joyous moments that had eluded me for so long. This time, I was stepping into the exhilarating world of dating—a realm that felt both thrilling and terrifying. As I began to peel back the layers of self-doubt that once clouded my self-perception, I gradually unveiled the beautiful, authentic person I truly was—a woman yearning to live freely and chase happiness with open arms.

After a significant time away, my friend Payal returned to Austin, her presence like a warm ray of sunshine on a cold winter's day. She had recently completed her PharmD degree, an accomplishment I admired deeply. Most weekends, we took to the vibrant streets of Austin, our laughter echoing off the city's lively backdrop as we explored new venues and cherished each other's company. Our nights were filled with adventure: discovering hidden gems in local eateries and dancing to the pulsating rhythms of live music. Meeting new people had always come naturally to me; I thrived in social settings, easily striking up conversations and forming connections that felt electric.

Amidst this whirlwind of social activity, I found myself casually seeing a guy named Chris. He was intriguing, but his heart seemed locked away, still haunted by the shadows of his past and the remnants of his ex-wife. In some ways, this emotional unavailability was a convenient shield for me—it allowed me to tread lightly in this budding relationship without the pressure of vulnerability. We enjoyed our time together, indulging in playful banter and casual outings, while I navigated my own feelings, grateful for the space to nurture my healing journey.

I found myself grappling with my weight once again, a familiar struggle that had plagued me for years. However, this time I was ready to take drastic measures—I had made the momentous decision to undergo surgery. I had heard about a groundbreaking laparoscopic procedure known as Lap-Band, designed to assist morbidly obese patients like myself in their weight loss journeys. This procedure involves placing an adjustable band around the upper portion of the stomach, creating a small pouch that restricts food intake. The magic of this band lies in its adjustability; a healthcare professional can loosen or tighten it by injecting or removing saline solution, customizing the restriction level to fit individual needs.

At 249 pounds, I met the qualifications for the procedure, supported by my medical insurance. The news that my surgery would be covered felt like a significant victory—a beacon of hope amid the darkness of my previous weight loss attempts, which had offered little success. I vividly remember counting down the days until surgery with a mix of anticipation and anxiety, each passing minute fueling my desire for change.

In preparation for the surgery, I was instructed to adhere to a strict liquid diet for two weeks prior to the procedure. It was a challenging adjustment, but I was determined to make it work. Miraculously, I managed to lose my first ten pounds before even stepping into the operating room—a small victory that kept me motivated.

On the day of the surgery, my partner Eddie took me to the hospital. The sterile environment was intimidating yet oddly comforting, knowing I was taking steps toward a healthier future. I remember the gentle hum of hospital machinery and the crisp scent of antiseptic in the air as I was taken back to the operating room. Eddie waited anxiously in the waiting area, his loyal presence a source of strength for me.

After the procedure, I was relieved to learn from the doctor that everything had gone wonderfully. He did, however, inform Eddie that he had to repair a hiatal hernia—a condition that had allowed a part of my stomach to push up through my diaphragm. This unexpected news gave me a moment of concern, but I knew it was something that needed to be addressed for my health. Afterward, I was required to stay overnight in the hospital, as per my insurance provider's policy, to ensure I received proper care during my recovery.

The next morning, Eddie returned to pick me up and help me transition back home, where my real journey of recovery would begin. I couldn't help but feel a surge of gratitude as I walked out of the hospital, aware that I was about to embark on a new chapter in my life.

As the weeks passed, I began to see the pounds melt away, and with each pound lost, a new sense of lightness washed over me. I started to feel noticeably better about myself and my body. By the time summer came to a close, I had shed nearly 80 pounds—an astonishing transformation that invigorated my spirit. I quickly realized I was experiencing feelings of fullness much more rapidly when eating, a clear sign that the surgery had significantly impacted my relationship with food. In my eyes, the venture into surgery had been an undeniable success, revitalizing not only my body but also my confidence and hope for the future.

On the bustling eve of Halloween, with an electric atmosphere buzzing through the streets, Payal and I decided to kick off our festivities at an eclectic bar nestled along South Congress. The air was filled with the laughter of costumed revelers and the faint sound of music spilling onto the sidewalk. As we entered, a warm glow from the dim lighting embraced us, beckoning us to indulge in the night's offerings.

We made our way to the bar and found seats beside a strikingly handsome, bald-headed man. His features were chiseled, his jawline strong, but there was an understated quality to his good looks that made him stand out without being overtly flashy—almost like a secret waiting to be discovered. Payal, with her charismatic aura and infectious laughter, quickly captured his attention, and they fell seamlessly into an animated conversation that seemed to envelop them in their own world.

I, on the other hand, sat there feeling increasingly invisible. It was frustrating; he barely acknowledged my presence, speaking just a few curt words in my direction before redirecting all his energy toward Payal. A surge of irritation boiled inside me. How could he overlook me when I had put so much effort into my appearance? That night, I wore a chic black baby doll turtleneck mini dress that hugged my figure perfectly, accentuating my curves while offering a touch of playful sophistication. Complementing my outfit were sleek, knee-high boots that clicked confidently against the wooden floor as I shifted in my seat. My short, layered bob, styled to perfection, framed my face elegantly. I felt stunning—radiant even—yet I was being eclipsed by a conversation that didn't include me.

After what felt like an eternity of watching them exchange smiles and lively banter, I decided I had enough. As we prepared to leave the bar, I summoned a mix of boldness and defiance. Leaning a little closer to the man, I flashed him a confident smile and handed him my business card. "Maybe you should call me sometime," I said, my voice steady despite the surge of emotions churning within me. Without waiting for a response or turning back for another glance, Payal and I strode out of the bar, ready to embrace whatever adventures awaited us on that vibrant Halloween night.

At 2 a.m., my phone buzzed softly, illuminating the darkened car with a warm glow. Heart racing with anticipation, I glanced at the screen to find his name flashing back at me. The message read, "How did I let your hot ass get away?" It struck me, resonating deep within my thoughts and feelings. I couldn't help but smile at the unexpected compliment—it was, after all, a sentiment I had shared. My fingers danced across the screen as I replied playfully, "I don't know, you must be dumb." His response was almost immediate: "When can I see you again?"

A thrill ran through me as I decided that the perfect place to meet would be Magnolia, my favorite after-bar haunt. It was a cozy, inviting restaurant that buzzed with life even in the early hours of the morning. Open twenty-four hours a day, it was known for its charming atmosphere and delicious comfort food. Most importantly, I craved my beloved Mag Mud—an indulgent dish of creamy, spicy queso topped with freshly diced pico de gallo and hearty black beans. Despite its name, which made it sound like mud, it tasted divine. It was truly a guilty pleasure of mine.

I arrived a little early, excitement bubbling inside me as I waited in the dimly lit lobby for a table to become available. The ambiance was a mixture of laughter from nearby tables and the sizzling sounds from the kitchen, creating an inviting backdrop to my growing anticipation.

Moments later, the door swung open, and he walked in, his presence filling the space with undeniable energy. I stood to greet him, my heart pounding as he closed the distance between us. Without hesitation, he leaned in and pressed his lips against mine—a kiss that sent an electrifying jolt through every nerve in my body. It was a moment charged with an unspoken connection, sealing our new beginning.

Soon, we were nestled in a cozy booth, the small space enveloping us in intimacy as we lost ourselves in conversation. Between kisses and laughter, the world around us faded away; it felt as if I had known him my entire life. We talked effortlessly, weaving our thoughts and dreams together amid the clinking of plates and the muffled voices of other patrons enjoying their late-night meals. I listened, captivated, as he shared his journey—working diligently on his dissertation for a PhD in Computational Linguistics at the prestigious University of Texas. I learned about his academic accolades, including an undergraduate degree from Princeton and an impressive collection of Master's degrees. He was undoubtedly accomplished, but what truly drew me in was his warmth and the genuine kindness that radiated from him.

From that magical night onward, we were inseparable. The thrill of being together filled my days with laughter and joy. As Thanksgiving approached, I decided it was time for him to meet my family—a daunting prospect that made my stomach flutter with anxiety. Would they accept him? After all, he was nearly ten years older than me and, at that moment, lacked a traditional career path. I imagined the potential reactions from my sisters and my mom, each of them full of opinions, and my heart raced at the thought.

Yet, as I gave him directions to my mother's house, we spoke with a tenderness that felt so natural. Just before we hung up, he surprised me with a heartfelt declaration: "I love you." A wave of emotions washed over me, and without a moment's hesitation, I returned the sentiment, "I love you too." The truth of my feelings rang clear—there was no doubt in my heart. I was in love with him, and the thought both thrilled and frightened me. This was the beginning of something beautiful, and I couldn't wait to see where it would lead us.

My mom was utterly smitten with him. He and she would engage in endless conversations that danced around literature and poetry—her favorite subjects, topics she could talk about for hours. Whenever he was around, it felt like a breath of fresh air had swept through our home, clearing the stale currents of routine and replacing them with the vibrant excitement of new ideas and shared passions. He had this remarkable ability to say what he meant and mean what he said, a rarity that made him all the more enchanting in my eyes.

It wasn't long before I had the chance to meet his parents, who lived in Tucson, Arizona. They had been divorced for quite some time, yet both welcomed me with open arms when Ben introduced me to them. I still remember the flutter of uncertainty in my stomach and the quiet worry that lingered in the back of my mind. Not wanting to be caught off guard, I leaned in and asked him if he had warned them that I was Black. He looked me straight in the eyes, his expression earnest and unwavering, and said with calm conviction, "Why? You're the woman I love, and they will love you because I love you." His words resonated deeply, striking a chord I never knew existed. Even though I was filled with nervous energy, knowing he was by my side made the daunting prospect of meeting his family feel not just manageable but almost exhilarating. I had never known a love quite like this before, and at that moment, I was all in.

Fast forward four years to Christmas 2015, and we still found ourselves living separately, traditions intact. It was once again time for my mom's annual Christmas Eve party, followed by the festive Christmas Day dinner, an occasion filled with laughter, warmth, and the smell of holiday treats wafting through the air. The sparkling lights and cheerful decorations adorned every corner of the house, setting the perfect atmosphere for celebration. My aunts Jaquelyn and Patricia were there, their laughter ringing out as we all gathered together, enjoying each other's company while waiting for dinner to start. I was tucked away in the study, chatting animatedly with my cousin Jadyn, lost in the warmth of family when I suddenly heard Ben's voice calling for me from the living room.

Curiosity piqued, I made my way towards him, my mind racing with questions about what he might want. We had already exchanged gifts that morning, leaving me blissfully unaware of any surprises still in store. When I entered the living room, what I saw took my breath away. Ben was on one knee, the glow of the Christmas lights reflecting in his eyes as he presented me with a stunning ring. In that moment, the world around us faded away; all I could hear was the cheer and excitement of my family as they erupted into joyful screams. Honestly, I couldn't even comprehend the words he uttered as my heart raced in my chest. In a heartbeat, I found myself responding with an emphatic "Yes!" before we wrapped each other in an embrace, the ring shimmering in his hand as if it held the light of our future within it. It was surreal, a moment I had never envisioned for myself. I had spent years believing that I wasn't the marrying kind, yet my love for him transcended all doubts and fears. The idea of spending a lifetime with Ben filled me with a profound sense of excitement—an eagerness for what lay ahead.

As the months rolled on, we took the plunge and moved in together, our lives merging as we prepared for our nuptials. I chuckled at the notion of "living in sin," but it felt like a small price to pay given that we were embarking on this thrilling journey toward marriage. The days were filled with joyful chaos as we balanced wedding planning with our demanding full-time jobs. I cherished my career as an Account Executive at a software company, and Ben, with his passion for innovation, was climbing the ranks as a Machine Learning and AI Scientist.

After much searching, we found the perfect venue for our wedding—a beautiful museum and sculpture garden nestled in downtown Austin. It was a place rich with artistry and culture, one we had frequented during our courtship. Its stunning architecture and lush landscape would serve as the magnificent backdrop for our special day. As we envisioned exchanging vows in such a breathtaking location, my heart swelled with gratitude and joy. We weren't just planning a wedding; we were crafting the beginning of a beautiful new chapter filled with love, creativity, and shared dreams.

Before we knew it, a year had sped by, and we found ourselves on the cusp of our long-anticipated big day. We had chosen April for our wedding, a month that promised a reprieve from the sweltering Texas heat. Our venue, with its enchanting outdoor setting, was perfect, with fresh spring blooms ensuring our celebration would be embraced by nature's splendor.

Months before the ceremony, I embarked on the exhilarating journey of dress shopping alone. I wanted to immerse myself in the moment, free from the weight of others' opinions. It was an empowering experience, standing in the hushed glow of the boutique, surrounded by shimmering fabrics and delicate lace. Here I was, a 37-year-old woman who had finally found the love of her life, reveling in the knowledge that my happiness was entirely in my hands. I embraced this newfound freedom, cherishing every moment of planning my wedding. I was producing this dream event on my own, deciding alongside Ben on every detail without relying on my parents for financial support. This was the liberation that comes with age—a stark contrast to the expectations of a bride in her twenties. It was a profound achievement, one of my life's greatest victories.

Our wedding day unfolded like a fairytale. The morning started with a curtain of rain pouring down, threatening to dampen my spirits. Panic bubbled within me, but Pam, my steadfast hairdresser since I was fourteen, was a calming presence amidst the chaos. She slipped into our cozy condo, transforming my hair while offering soothing words as the rain drummed insistently against the windows.

"It will stop," she assured me, her voice steady. "Nothing is going to ruin this moment." Miraculously, her words seemed to summon a change in the skies. The rain ceased, and the sun emerged with vibrant intensity, illuminating everything around us. By the time we arrived at the garden, the air was refreshing, a perfect 80 degrees, and the ground beneath my feet was dry, as if the heavens had conspired to grant us the most beautiful day imaginable. My heart swelled with joy.

I applied my makeup with ease, feeling composed, until the photographer I had carefully chosen interjected. "You need lipstick," she insisted. "Otherwise, you'll look washed out in your photos." With a mix of reluctance and curiosity, I followed her advice. In the end, I was grateful; the photographs captured the essence of our day brilliantly.

The moment I had been waiting for arrived at last: I hadn't seen Ben since the previous evening, and the anticipation was electric as I caught sight of him standing under the grand awning at the end of the aisle. I slipped into my elegant Zac Posen gown, fastening the intricate jewelry and donning my stunning Badgley Mischka heels. Surprisingly, I felt grounded and calm. Surrounded by my mother, sisters, Payal, and Pam, it felt as if the universe had aligned, placing me exactly where I was meant to be. A wave of tranquility washed over me; I was ready to embrace this new chapter of my life.

The ceremony flowed seamlessly, the weather holding up beautifully, while all 75 of our cherished guests reveled in the joyous atmosphere. Ben and I basked in our happiness, dancing through the night as if the world had faded away. When the reception finally drew to a close, we made our way back to our condo, our hearts still soaring. We hurriedly packed for our long-awaited adventure in Rome, Italy, with a 6 AM flight on the horizon. In hindsight, perhaps we should have indulged in an extra day of rest before our honeymoon—the exhaustion can be overwhelming after such a whirlwind. Yet, in that blissful moment, we felt an incredible wave of happiness as we stepped into our new journey as a married couple.

We drifted into a deep sleep for most of our flight to Rome, the gentle hum of the airplane engine lulling us toward our adventure—a twelve-day cruise through the sun-kissed Mediterranean. Upon landing at the bustling Leonardo Da Vinci Fiumicino Airport, we hopped into a taxi that whisked us away to Civitavecchia, a quaint coastal town adorned with charming cobblestone streets and vibrant cafés, where we would board our MSC cruise. After a brief check-in at our cozy hotel for a single night's stay before continuing our journey to Genoa, Italy, we stepped outside to immerse ourselves in the beauty of Civitavecchia. The town was a picturesque blend of historic architecture and sparkling blue vistas; there was so much to explore, and we had only sixteen short hours to soak it all in.

We strolled leisurely through the city center, absorbing the sights and sounds around us. The aroma of fresh bread and rich Italian cuisine wafted through the air, drawing us into a delightful restaurant where we savored a magnificent lunch, the flavors bursting with authenticity. After our meal, we retreated to our room, the exhaustion from our travels finally catching up with us. Ben, having barely slept the night before our departure, reveled in the comfort of a soft bed, while I, still electrified from the excitement of the day, reluctantly succumbed to sleep.

The next morning arrived with a soft golden glow as we prepared to embark on our grand adventure. The scorching heat greeted us as we stepped outside, but the anticipation of what awaited us at the ship's dock made every bead of sweat worthwhile. As we entered the grandeur of the cruise ship, its beauty took our breath away. A friendly steward promptly whisked our luggage away, leaving us to explore. When we finally reached our suite, our eyes widened at the sight—fresh roses delicately arranged on the bed and a chilled bottle of champagne glistening in the sunlight on the table. It felt surreal. The ship buzzed with life, offering a cornucopia of restaurants, dazzling shows, and vibrant clubs designed to entertain and enchant guests from around the world. Amidst the diverse crowd, we felt like we were on a secluded island together, surrounded by foreign accents.

Ben, fluent in five languages, and I found ourselves captivated by a different language—the language of love. After five years of growing together, we were rediscovering each other, talking for hours and stealing moments of passion beneath the stars.

Yet, in what felt like a whirlwind, we made the hasty decision to enter escrow for our first home together, closing on the seventh day of the cruise. While this was undeniably thrilling, a wave of concern washed over me as I contemplated packing, moving, and the challenges of juggling a full-time job all at once. I had just started an Account Executive position at an emerging start-up in downtown Austin. Even as we celebrated this exciting new chapter, the looming task of relocating felt overwhelming. Despite the chaos, we eventually cocooned ourselves into the warmth of our new home nestled in the heart of East Downtown Austin.

But amidst the everyday rhythms of life, something still felt amiss. No, it wasn't the prospect of children—Ben and I had long decided that parenthood wasn't in our cards. Our joy stemmed from our adventures together, having traveled to enchanting places like Paris, Spain, Chile, Costa Rica, and back to Italy. We were living our dream. Yet, a nagging sense of dissatisfaction lingered within me. My job, while stable, lacked fulfillment, and I sensed I had reached a glass ceiling—so close, yet unreachable due to my lack of a college degree.

With a flutter of nerves, I broached the idea of returning to school with Ben. Would he think I was chasing something foolish? I was a 39-year-old sales executive, who, after nearly two decades away from the academic grind, wondered if I could realistically step back into the role of a full-time student. Yet, to my relief, he radiated confidence in me, fully supporting my aspiration without a hint of doubt or fear of failure. I was immensely grateful for his belief in me, but now I faced the daunting task of fostering that same confidence within myself.

I took the plunge—quitting my job at the start-up and embracing the early morning light as I enrolled at Texas State University, the very institution where my academic journey had begun at the tender age of seventeen. With renewed determination, I decided to double major in Advertising and Mass Communication, feeling a swirl of excitement and apprehension as the dawn of 2019 marked the beginning of this transformative chapter in my life.

CHAPTER 7

THE NEXT CHAPTER

As I stepped onto the vibrant campus of Texas State University, a wave of exhilaration washed over me, igniting a renewed sense of purpose deep within my chest. I was once again a proud Bobcat. As I climbed the long, worn flight of stairs leading to Old Main, the Communications Building, every step felt invigorating. The sun bathed the historic façade in a warm glow, highlighting the memories and dreams that lingered in its shadow. Glancing around, I couldn't help but notice how I stood out among the students bustling about, brimming with youthful energy and ambition. With my silver hair and mature demeanor, I clearly resembled the wise elder on campus, navigating a sea of eager nineteen- and twenty-year-olds.

But rather than feel out of place, my age served as a humbling advantage. These young scholars, with their innocent enthusiasm, were still navigating the confusing labyrinth of their futures, while I had a clear and defined vision of my own path. I was determined to wield my degree as a key to unlocking better-paying job opportunities— positions that had once seemed unattainable due to my lack of a college education.

My routine became a rhythm of determination, commuting from Austin to San Marcos three days a week— Monday, Tuesday, and Thursday. Each trek was a deliberate act, pacing myself toward the goal of completing my degree in just one year. Within the lively walls of my communications classes, I encountered a fascinating group of minds. The students around me were bursting with dreams, ambition, and that unmistakable spark of youthful hope. There was a time when I, too, had shared those fiery aspirations, and it rekindled my passion to strive for more, both in life and in my career.

Then, like a cruel twist of fate, the world changed. Just two months shy of my graduation, the shadow of COVID-19 descended upon us, transforming our lives and dreams in an instant. After so many years of waiting and working toward this moment, I found that there would be no grand ceremony to celebrate my achievement. Instead, the palpable excitement of walking across the stage in a cap and gown was replaced by the stark reality of a postponed graduation. The diploma that represented years of hard work and perseverance arrived in my mailbox a month after finals—a bittersweet acknowledgment of my journey. I was thrilled to hold it in my hands, yet the absence of celebration left me yearning for the fanfare and recognition of this monumental milestone.

Amidst this whirlwind of change, I began experiencing troubling complications with my Lap-Band. The once-promising solution to my weight struggles had turned into a nightmare; I found myself unable to eat anything without it immediately rebelling against me. It felt as if my body was turning against its own survival, forcing me into a cycle reminiscent of anorexia and bulimia. The prospect of continuing down this path became unbearable, and deep down, I knew I would eventually require a reversal surgery. A gnawing fear gripped me—what if all my hard work led to the weight crashing back down upon me, rendering my struggle pointless? In a moment of resolve during the surgery, I instructed my doctor to perform a gastric sleeve procedure, which would remove a significant portion of my stomach to help prevent excessive weight gain.

Yet, the battle raged on. I was constantly confronted by feelings of discontent as the scale began to reflect minor weight gains—not alarming, but enough to stir concern. I had achieved considerable weight loss, but the presence of excess skin around my midsection lingered, a reminder of the journey I had traversed. Months after the reversal, I underwent another surgery—a tummy tuck that lasted five arduous hours and was accompanied by a recovery experience that felt like wading through molasses. However, the final results were worth every moment of discomfort. My doctor meticulously crafted a new belly button, and seeing it for the first time was surreal, almost like opening a door to a body I had never truly known.

Finally, I stood before the mirror, a stranger in my own skin, filled with a sense of wonder as I slipped into a bikini for the very first time. The joy, the exhilaration—I was over the moon. After years of struggle, I had emerged transformed and unwavering, ready to embrace the life that awaited me.

I wasted no time figuring out my next move. The thrill of applying to jobs as a college graduate was incredible. Finally, I could let my imposter syndrome go and know that I was truly qualified for the roles I was applying to. Soon after, I received an email from a marketing and SEO company in Seattle, inviting me to interview for a new department they were building. They wanted me to be their inaugural Director of Customer Success, tasked with hiring and training a team of Customer Success Managers. I was elated. It was a fully remote position, and I began working from my home office just a month after receiving my degree. After being unemployed for a year, I was excited to rejoin the workforce—as a Director, no less.

The feelings of inadequacy were hard to shake as I built the team from the ground up, created KPIs (key performance indicators), and streamlined our standard operating procedures. But I was having a blast doing what I loved and was determined to excel. Unfortunately, the company experienced a downturn due to the pandemic. After a year, they decided to eliminate my department. Letting go of my team—and myself—was the hardest thing I had faced in my career. However, I dusted myself off and dove back into the job hunt.

I didn't have to search for long. Within two months, I was interviewing for a Senior Director of Sales position at a payments company in Austin. They specialized in legal payments processing for attorneys and law firms, which I knew nothing about. But I did know how to sell and how to lead others to success in sales. The pay was incredible, and I accepted the offer after being impressed by their HR team. Although I was nervous to start, I knew I had the experience and ideas to back me up.

Things were going well at first. I traveled up to three times a month for trade shows and conferences, stepping in whenever my small team needed extra support. I loved every minute of it. I was contributing to the company's bottom line, and my team was performing well. My two verticals were thriving, and I was excited about my future with the company.

However, things began to change after we acquired another company. I found myself reporting to a new boss I wasn't too keen on, and the company's goals began shifting. The acquired company clearly had leverage and a great product we needed to stay competitive, but it was clear that my future there was uncertain. After two years and a few months, I knew it was time to make my exit. Although I didn't have anything lined up, I left with a generous severance package and cashed in my equity share of the company. I felt secure and confident, knowing I had gained valuable, marketable skills since graduating.

Two weeks later, I started my role as Director of Inside Sales at a small managed services company based in Texas. There would be less travel, but I had to be in the office much more frequently. After being spoiled by remote jobs for so long, it took some getting used to.

I settled in just fine, loving my team, which was full of young salespeople who reminded me of myself when I first started in sales. But I soon felt out of my depth and began to lose confidence. I had been there for just five months when my mother passed away. Everything leading up to that moment seemed arbitrary. I knew what I had to do: I had to leave. I was unhappy, unfulfilled, and, sadly, miserable. More importantly, I needed to give myself the space to grieve.

There are no decent handbooks available to guide you through the murky waters of career unfulfillment—at least, none that captured my interest or resonated with my predicament. I found myself yearning for a path that ignited passion within me, a calling that felt aligned with my spirit. My mother wouldn't want me to languish in a job that stifled my ambitions and dreams. I could no longer ignore the gnawing ache in my chest; staying in that role felt like a betrayal of my very essence. My soul was crying out for liberation, and deep down, I knew my work had suffered under the weight of my dissatisfaction—it was as clear to me as smudged ink on a once-blank page.

Parting ways with the familiar was an emotional labyrinth, fraught with uncertainty yet tinged with necessity. I clung to my fears, unsure of what lay ahead. The shadow of doubt crept in as I ruminated on the myriad career opportunities that had slipped through my fingers like grains of sand. Adding to my turmoil, Ben, too, had exited his job of eight years, spurred by the unbearable tension between work and life. Now, we found ourselves adrift, both temporarily unanchored from our careers.

Though we had a comfortable nest egg stowed away, I started to feel the strain after a year of inactivity. A creeping unease settled over me, forcing me to confront the wavering ambition flickering within Ben. Our intimacy had dwindled, and I felt an insatiable annoyance boil inside me each time I glanced in his direction. It was painfully clear that life had transformed into a chaotic garden, where the weeds of frustration and doubt overshadowed any budding joy. I stood at a pivotal crossroads, grappling with my inner turmoil and embarking on a profound journey of introspection. There had to be something out there that could rekindle my spirit.

While Ben remained the love of my life, I was aware that every marriage experiences ups and downs. Tough times, I told myself, were merely seasons, and I had faith that our relationship could weather this storm. To reclaim my sense of self, I turned once again to painting—a passion that pulsed through my veins and was woven into the very fabric of my being. Art had always been a bridge between Ben and me; we often lost ourselves in the vibrant energy of gallery openings that dotted the art scene in Austin. Years before our paths intertwined, I had even held a group show, showcasing my artwork and aspirations to the world. Engaging with art was more than a pastime; it was a lifeline, a way to breathe life into the shadows that seemed to envelop my existence. It was time to immerse myself in the colors and emotions that could truly fulfill me once more.

I found myself applying for jobs in every direction, casting my net wide with hope. Yet, despite scoring a handful of interviews, none of these opportunities materialized into solid offers. It felt as though my once-thriving streak of success in securing employment had come to an abrupt and disheartening halt. As despair crept in, I stumbled upon the therapeutic power of journaling. Words flowed from my fingertips like an unbroken stream, spilling onto the page as I wrote, wrote, and wrote some more. Just like my mother, I discovered a deep-seated passion for literature that had long been nestled within me, particularly for the beauty and emotion of poetry. I recalled the thrill of reciting my verses at family gatherings and how the warm smiles and encouraging nods from my loved ones filled me with a sense of pride and purpose. But how could I transform this joy into a sustainable career? The reality struck me: writers often struggle to make a decent living unless they achieve the coveted status of being published, and I felt utterly lost about where to begin this daunting journey. I realized I had to aim high, reintroduce myself to the world, and declare my potential to those around me—and, more importantly, to prove to myself that I was indeed capable of achieving greatness. Thus, I committed to writing diligently, seeking an outlet to channel my swirling emotions and unvoiced dreams onto the page.

CHAPTER 8

GOING BACK

To truly grasp the depths of my despair at just 24 years old, I had to revisit the tapestry of my childhood, woven with both comfort and confusion. During therapy, I diligently explored my past, striving to confront the shadows that haunted me. It became essential to unravel the reasons behind my sudden crash into emotional turmoil—a wall I collided with at extraordinary speed.

Reflecting on my upbringing, I realize that, on the surface, it seemed quite decent. I was blessed with nurturing, loving parents. My mother dedicated herself fully to our family, placing her career on hold to raise four children. My father, Eddie, often vanished into the world of soldiers, absorbed by the duties of military life, far from home. Despite frequent relocations, I never felt unmoored. My mom had an uncanny ability to create a sense of stability and warmth in every new house.

No matter how sudden the move, the moment we stepped through the front door of a new place, our rooms felt like home. She worked tirelessly to ensure our creature comforts—our toys, books, and familiar belongings—were unpacked and arranged in no time. Each transition was handled with near-magical ease, as she recognized the challenges we faced: new neighborhoods, unfamiliar schools, and the daunting task of making new friends. Her proactive nature made those upheavals manageable; she was our steady anchor amid the chaos.

After a long day at school, we came home to her welcoming embrace and the enticing aroma of an after-school snack wafting from the kitchen. We tackled our homework together, her comforting presence beside us as we studied. Dinner was a family affair, filled with laughter and stories. As the day waned, we settled into our nightly rituals—bathing, brushing our teeth, and sharing whispered secrets beneath the covers. Mom would make her rounds, tucking us in with a gentle kiss and a reassuring smile. Her love was expressed through soft gestures rather than overt affection.

In contrast, Eddie exuded warmth and affection. When he was home, I often found myself outside with him, surrounded by the scent of barbecued meat as we worked on the family station wagon. In the evenings, we would retreat to his music room, where the strains of his favorite songs filled the air like a warm embrace, and the world outside faded away.

Growing up in Germany offered me a kaleidoscopic view of life, subtly teaching me that existence was not merely black and white. With a stroke of luck, I learned to see the world in vibrant color. Perhaps that's why it felt so natural for me to date and fall in love with a white Jewish guy from Tucson; our differences melted away, revealing the underlying connections that united us.

Yet, that journey wasn't without reservations. During my dad's first tour in Desert Storm, I faced countless challenges at the school my mom had chosen for us—the same institution where she had once been a student herself. Each day was an uphill battle. My fiercest tormentor, Melody, delighted in turning my school days into a living nightmare. From knocking my books from my grasp to tripping me without hesitation, she would stop at nothing to demean me, even locking me in a bathroom stall. I remember the sound of my own screams echoing off the walls, tears streaming down my cheeks, until a teacher's assistant arrived and chased off Melody and her crew.

"Do not give them the power to see you cry," the assistant asserted fiercely. "They think they've won. Find a way to reclaim your power." Her words washed over me like a lifeboat in a stormy sea. I clung to them desperately, hoping to find my footing once more. No longer would I care if my peers mistook my love for literature or my articulate manner of speaking as snobbery. I didn't have a southern drawl; I spoke with clarity and passion for learning. I wasn't the teacher's pet out of favoritism—I earned that distinction through my dedication and respect for knowledge. These traits didn't render me an outcast; they illuminated a truth about myself, helping me navigate the turbulent currents of adolescence with self-awareness and quiet resilience.

I vividly remember the day the bullying became too much. I was sitting down in the cafeteria, about to eat with my class, when I saw Dionne from across the room. She was in a different class, and each group had to sit together for lunch and assemblies. I was so happy to see my twin sister, but I didn't dare look up, afraid it would spark more insults from Melody. I peeked at Dionne through my eyelashes, and we locked eyes. Dionne smiled brightly and placed her index finger under her chin, signaling for me to keep my head up. I immediately burst into tears. Years later, I told Dionne how much it meant to see her cheering me on, knowing she was in my corner and always would be.

Things continued much as they had since I started at Radium Springs Elementary until summer break finally arrived, and we rounded out the year with Field Day. It was a day reserved for outdoor fun and games. I brought a blanket from home, found a spot away from the activities, rolled it out, and sat cross-legged, reading one of my favorite books, The Lion, the Witch and the Wardrobe by C.S. Lewis. The teaching assistant walked over and asked if she could join me. She sat down on the blanket, asked what I was reading, and we made small talk.

"You know," she said, "It won't always be like this. Eventually, you will find your way." Then she quietly asked, "Are you sure you don't want to play with the other kids?"

Without hesitation, I replied, "There's no point. They hate me."

"Oh, sweetheart, they can't hate you. They don't even know you."

I remember thinking how odd it was that she said that to me. Isn't that exactly what racism stems from—a lack of understanding about someone? Hating what you don't know or understand? Those kids certainly didn't like me, and I was no longer interested in finding out why. I had no fight left in me, and one thing that gave me solace was knowing we wouldn't be in this town and around these intolerable kids for much longer. We would soon be PCS'ing to another base, this time in Louisiana. PCS is a military acronym for Permanent Change of Station, meaning moving from one duty station to another. I was relieved that I didn't have to stay in Georgia over the summer. We would be moving right before the summer break ended and starting at a new school.

We were stationed at Fort Polk, nestled near the quaint town of Leesville, Louisiana, where the warm, humid air clung to your skin and the sounds of cicadas filled the evening quiet. While I was embracing this new chapter, my brother Terry remained behind in Georgia, diligently finishing his senior year among familiar faces and places. My sister Ylencia prepared for her sophomore year, full of potential and uncharted experiences, while Dionne and I geared up for the transition to middle school, entering eighth grade with a mix of excitement and trepidation.

This summer—though it lacked the shimmering allure of youth often depicted in films—marked a significant turning point for me. It was the summer I began to discover my voice, not just literally, but within myself. As a member of the school choir, I eagerly anticipated each practice, losing myself in the harmonies and uplifting lyrics. Mom, my steadfast supporter, would pick me up after practice, and together we settled into a comforting rhythm that made each day feel a little brighter.

Yet, while I flourished in this new environment, Dionne struggled. She had undergone back surgery the previous year and was confined to a rigid brace that encased her torso from collarbone to hip. The sleek, cold material contrasted sharply with her spirited personality, leaving her feeling trapped and miserable. She had to wear it for a year and a half, a burden that weighed heavily on her young shoulders.

At school, her condition often drew curiosity, with classmates asking questions about her brace and recovery. Amazingly, Dionne handled their inquiries with a grace beyond her years, effortlessly turning potentially uncomfortable moments into opportunities for connection. She made friends easily, and to my immense relief, she didn't endure the teasing or bullying that haunted my memories. I was thankful for that; no child should have to face harsh judgment or cruel remarks, especially when I had felt their sting so keenly.

I often wondered why I had been the target of such unwarranted animosity. What was so deeply flawed within me to warrant such disdain? My mind spiraled with self-doubt until my mom offered her perspective: "They're just jealous of you." Her words, though meant to be comforting, struck me as peculiar. I didn't feel special—I longed to be just like everyone else.

Sensing my uncertainty, she would remind me, "You are not like everyone else. You are special, and they want to be like you. We usually dislike others for what we see as their strengths—it's a reflection of their insecurities, not yours. Never dim your light for anyone." Her wise words echoed in my mind, guiding me through the turbulent waters of adolescence and into adulthood. Mom's rare, prophetic advice always had a way of soothing my restless heart.

Our time in Louisiana unfolded over three transformative years. Before long, a new chapter awaited us at Fort Hood, Texas, the final military post of my father's long and commendable career. After 27 years of devoted service, Eddie made the momentous decision to retire—an achievement worth celebrating amidst the transitions. Our move unfolded yet again in the sweltering summer heat, and soon the horizon of high school loomed for both Dionne and me. Meanwhile, Ylencia faced her own milestone, embarking on her senior year at Ellison High School, excited for her impending journey to Baylor in the fall.

Dionne had been busy over the summer and had found herself a boyfriend. They were glued to each other, and she and I began to drift apart. Guys didn't look at me—they never had. When the three of us walked into Ellison for the first time, Dionne went off with her boyfriend and said I couldn't hang out with them and the rest of the football team, which was full of all the popular kids. I was stunned and hurt. She was my sister, my twin, and even she was rejecting me. I walked away and sat on the floor in the Band/Choir hallway before classes started. I had brought a book that I pretended to read as I cried.

As the year progressed, I found my own circle of friends and joined the Student Council and Yearbook Club. I was doing what I loved—writing, taking pictures, and interviewing for the yearbook. I was finally in my groove, though I didn't have much of a social life. That was fine; I spent my weekends reading and not really doing much of anything.

Time flew by, and before I knew it, it was our senior year. Ylencia had been away at college for nearly three years by that point, and I was now the Yearbook co-editor. Working on the theme for the yearbook became an obsession. I worked on page layouts, cropped photos, and approved stories. It was so much fun for me. That's when I realized that I loved to lead and was good at it. I suppose that experience led me down the path to becoming a director for many tech companies later in life.

However, my rise up the ranks wasn't without obstacles. I often felt invisible and undervalued—something I'm sure many Black people in positions of power have faced. I made it a point to look around in every meeting, searching to see if anyone looked like me. There seldom was. I couldn't help but wonder if I was hired for a leadership position simply for the sake of diversity. I always felt the need to prove myself. I didn't have the liberty of being mediocre—I had to be ten times better than my White female and male counterparts. Corporate America is run by the Patriarchy, and I had to fight to find my voice and to know that what I brought to the table wasn't tied to the color of my skin.

It was a hard truth to grapple with, and I loathed this aspect of tech sales. It was daunting, trying to prove myself over and over again. I was proud of how far I had come, but after Mom's death, I no longer had the energy to pretend. I no longer had the mental capacity to capitulate to other people's expectations. I took a much-needed break to find what would truly make me happy.

Reflecting on my journey from that lonely moment in the Band hallway to becoming Yearbook co-editor, I see how pivotal those experiences were in shaping my resilience and ambition. Dionne's rejection stung deeply, but it catalyzed my growth. Finding my own circle of friends and pursuing my passions not only filled the void left by my sister, but also laid the groundwork for my future.

Entering senior year, I was fully immersed in creativity and leadership. The yearbook project became my sanctuary, a space where I could express myself and hone my skills. It was in this environment that I discovered my passion for leading—a passion that would eventually guide me in my career.

Now, as I stand at a crossroads, I understand the importance of pausing to reassess my path. This chapter may close with uncertainty, but it leaves me with a determination to seek what genuinely brings me happiness. The journey ahead is daunting, but I am ready to embrace it, armed with the lessons of my past and a newfound clarity about my worth.

CHAPTER 9

YOU MIGHT WIN

It was summer again, five months since my mom's departure from Earth. I thought of her often and found myself reaching for the phone, wanting to call her. It was muscle memory, really. Whenever something happened, big or small, I would always call her. She would feign annoyance at my constant calls, but I knew better. She loved me, and no matter how needy I was, I knew she would always drop what she was doing to talk to me.

I struggled to figure out my next move. I didn't know whether to return to Corporate America or not. I had always been able to land my next role. In fact, it was a running joke among my family members. They would say, "Diandra always finds a good job." But it seemed that my luck had run out. I was applying to jobs every day, only to receive rejection letters. I had to do some deep introspection. While I waited for the phone to ring, I took on consulting work in my field to bring in income. I was good at giving others advice and briefly entertained starting my own consulting business related to my expertise in sales and sales leadership. But standing up this business would take a lot, and I hit a wall of self-doubt.

Grief is a tricky thing. I didn't want to be happy. I wanted to wallow in it. Feelings of guilt for being here when Mom and Shawn were not began to take over. There was no easy way to navigate the pangs of guilt. One thing I knew for certain was that there was never going to be enough time.

There was never going to be enough time to do all that I wanted to do and be all that I wanted to be. Time is precious and ever fleeting, and I couldn't help but feel that my mom gave up on life. She threw in the towel, and I wanted to understand why. Her death came as such a shock because she was rarely ever sick. I never saw her in bed due to illness; she just always kept going. But then, she stopped. She bowed out. The autopsy results offered no help. It simply stated that she had hypertension and that was the ultimate cause of her death. I think I would have been more at peace if they had said she had suffered a heart attack. It would have made more sense.

When it comes down to it, I somehow felt that my mom had a choice—whether to stay or be welcomed to the other side. She chose what was right for her, and that brings me peace. Knowing that she ultimately made a decision for herself provides some consolation. For the first time in her life as a mom, grandmother, and sister, she did something "selfish," and for that, I find some comfort. I am, of course, sad that she is no longer here, but I am also glad that she finally got to do something just for her. What a way to go out.

It's often said there's no handbook on dealing with death. You just have to go through it before you can ever come to terms with it, and the idea of getting over it seems unimaginable. In essence, one has to move toward the pain to get through it and, hopefully, come out clean on the other side. My mom mourned her mother's death for the rest of her life. I remember one sunny day, sitting in my living room when my mom came to visit. We were just sitting there, watching TV before heading out to lunch, and she recalled a story about her mother and began to cry. All I could say was, "Oh, Mom. She's here with you. She's here with us. It's going to be okay." Just as quickly as those words left my lips, the television turned off. Neither of us had touched the remote, which was sitting on the coffee table. I was alarmed, but Mom wasn't.

She quipped, "That's just your grandma telling me to quit crying and go enjoy the day with my daughter."

That was the beauty of my mom. She could take any situation and make it light-hearted, more palatable for consumption, if you will. It was nearing the six-month mark, and how I missed hearing her laugh and seeing her smile. I was angry—boy, was I angry. In those six short months, we had experienced the birth of her great-granddaughter, our first Mother's Day without her, and soon we would be facing the holiday season without her too. I didn't know how we were going to make it through, but I had faith. We were all strong because of her, and together, we could get through anything.

It had been nearly four months since I'd quit my job, and I was starting to panic about my next move. Again. Nothing was working out. I'd had several interviews, but more often than not, I was being ghosted by recruiters and hiring managers alike. I couldn't figure out what I was doing wrong. There had been a slew of corporate layoffs in the technology space, so the market was saturated. I didn't know whether to start my own business, go back to school, or just wait it out. In the meantime, all I did was think—reevaluate my life choices and lament how foolish I was to quit my job in such an unstable economy.

Then I tapped into my faith and realized I had to give all these thoughts—all the ruminating—to God. The moment I decided that, I stopped caring about the missteps that had landed me in this position. I knew that what was meant to be would be. I was willing to ride the wave and relinquish whatever control I thought I had—that's the beauty of faith. It allows you the freedom of ignorance. I just knew everything would work out. I only had to be patient with myself and, more importantly, with God. I'm by no means a religious person, but I'm thankful that I have faith, even if it's just a tiny drop. I had faith that my life wouldn't always be in a state of upheaval. I trusted that this time in my life would make me more aware, more appreciative of all the blessings I'd been given. I had the best mom I could have ever asked for, and I had my siblings, my father, and my friends.

Undoubtedly, the void of losing her had changed me. I just hoped it had changed me for the better, and all I could do was allow time to tell.

As I stood on the precipice of uncertainty, I felt the weight of my mother's love guiding me. Though her laughter was absent, her spirit lived on in my heart, reminding me that every storm eventually passes. I was ready to embrace the unknown, trusting that this chapter of my life—filled with both sorrow and hope—was merely a stepping stone to something greater. With faith as my anchor, I knew I could navigate the waves ahead, one day at a time.

I decided it was time to embark on a new chapter in my therapy journey, one where I could deeply explore my struggles with body image. After some research, I found a therapist who specialized in this area of mental health, and I eagerly scheduled a meeting to see if she'd be the right fit. When I arrived, I was greeted by Rebecca. Her warm smile and inviting demeanor instantly put me at ease. She guided our conversation with thoughtful questions, but she also had a remarkable ability to let me speak freely, creating a space where my thoughts flowed unencumbered. I found myself sharing profound insights about my upbringing, recounting pivotal moments from my formative years, and reflecting on the challenges I faced in early adulthood. With each word, a sense of safety enveloped me, and before I knew it, we had developed a swift and genuine bond.

Encouraging yet gentle, Rebecca nudged me to confront the tangled mess of my feelings—my lingering self-loathing and insecurities—and together, we began to face the harsh truths that had long been buried beneath the surface.

As our sessions progressed, I started to recognize patterns in my thoughts and behaviors that I had previously overlooked. Rebecca introduced me to various therapeutic techniques, including mindfulness exercises and cognitive restructuring, which helped me challenge the negative beliefs I held about my body. With each new tool I learned, I felt a flicker of hope emerge, illuminating the darkness that had surrounded my self-image for so long.

We also explored the societal pressures and unrealistic standards of beauty that had seeped into my perceptions. Our discussions made me realize how deeply these external influences had shaped my thoughts, fueling a relentless cycle of comparison and self-criticism. Armed with this understanding, I began to identify moments when I was particularly hard on myself, and Rebecca encouraged me to practice self-compassion and reframe my inner dialogue.

One day, Rebecca introduced the concept of 'body neutrality'—an approach that urged me to focus on what my body could do rather than how it looked. This idea resonated with me, and I began to see my body in a new light. Instead of fixating on imperfections, I started to appreciate my body's strength and its resilience in carrying me through life's challenges. Each session became a stepping stone toward a healthier relationship with myself, allowing me to redefine beauty on my own terms.

As I dove deeper into this journey, I realized that it wasn't just about changing my outward perception but also about fortifying my inner self. I left each session feeling lighter and empowered by the knowledge that I wasn't alone in my struggles, fueled by an unwavering desire to cultivate acceptance and love for the person I am—both inside and out.

CHAPTER 10

THE PRESENT

Relearning how to live after losing someone so profoundly close to my heart feels like navigating through an interminable fog that clings to every thought, every breath. It's a chilling, dense mist that distorts reality, making the world around me seem darker and more surreal. The air is thick with an insidious heaviness, and every step feels laborious, burdened by the weight of absence. It's an overwhelming challenge to continue existing when a vital part of you—a piece of your very soul—has been ripped away without warning. I often liken this gut-wrenching experience to losing a leg in a tragic accident; suddenly, you find yourself relearning the simplest, most fundamental acts of living—like walking—haunted by the profound absence that once provided balance and stability.

Many amputees grapple with Phantom Limb Syndrome, where they still feel sensations or even gnawing pain in the place where their lost limb once was. This concept resonates deeply with me, as it perfectly encapsulates my experience after her untimely death. Though she was irrevocably gone from this world, I could still feel her presence surrounding me, like a warm, ethereal glow in the midst of darkness. The memory of her laughter reverberated in my mind, and her spirit haunted the corners of my home, reminding me of what was lost. The task of forging a new existence without her loomed dauntingly ahead—a monumental hill that seemed impossible to climb.

So, I rallied. I dug deep within myself, mustering every ounce of strength as if my very survival depended on it. Typically, I pride myself on being a resilient individual, stoic in the face of adversity. It came as no surprise that I hadn't shed a tear since my mother's passing—not out of a lack of hurt, but from the sheer effort to hold myself together. Yet, I knew I had to confront my emotional state head-on. My lack of visible grief didn't equate to an absence of mourning. This realization started to illuminate a hidden strength within me—a quiet resilience that began to bubble to the surface.

Despite this newfound awareness, the work ahead felt immense and overwhelming. Grief had unconsciously taken a toll on my nervous system, sending me spiraling into a state of perpetual worry, catastrophizing every aspect of my life. It felt like being trapped in a cage of anxiety, each bar forged from fear and doubt. If my sister didn't answer the phone on the first ring, I'd call her repeatedly, each unanswered call carving deeper into my anxiety until I imagined the worst possible scenarios unfolding. If Ben took a little too long on an errand, my heart would race, and panic would bubble up within me, conjuring nightmarish visions of accidents, illness, and loss. It was as if I had already been living in fear before her death, imagining countless ways she might slip away from me. I granted myself permission to cry only after I had fully imagined these disastrous outcomes, believing that if I braced for the worst, perhaps it would spare me some pain. But when the moment finally came—when I lost her—the raw agony was more than I could bear, a weight far heavier than any imagined scenario.

In the depths of my grief, I surrounded myself with tangible reminders of her existence, desperate to keep her spirit close. I purchased a delicate ring containing her ashes, nestled thoughtfully at its center—a constant reminder of her essence intertwined with my own. I also acquired a tiny bracelet designed to reveal her smiling picture when held to the light—a cherished treasure I could carry with me everywhere. These tokens brought brief moments of solace, a sense of comfort that would wash over me in waves, allowing me to feel her presence, tangible yet elusive, even in her absence. My home quickly transformed into a shrine of sorts, filled with her essence. Photographs adorned the walls—captured memories of joyous smiles and exuberant moments—and in the foyer, her urn took center stage beside the cherished book we had poured our hearts into together, along with an award she had received for excellence in teaching. She was everywhere, her spirit woven into the fabric of my days; yet, amidst all this, I still felt an aching emptiness—an enormous void that could not be filled. Each night, I prayed earnestly for her to visit me in my dreams, yearning for a sense of connection. Yet she rarely appeared, leaving me feeling lost and adrift, like a ship without a sail.

I remembered one of my former employees mentioning a medium he had consulted in Florida who had brought him some peace after he lost his father. He suggested I reach out to this medium, who had no online presence, thriving purely on word-of-mouth—an enigma in a digital world. With a blend of skepticism and hope, I scheduled a session, fervently hoping for a breakthrough—a tangible connection to my mother's spirit that might bring me the peace I so desperately sought. When we spoke for an hour, my heart was heavy with expectation, longing for a sign that could tether my disoriented soul to hers once more. Instead, I left the conversation feeling more frustrated than enlightened. Though it was comforting to converse with someone who knew nothing of my pain but offered an open ear, I found myself burdened with an insatiable need for reassurance. I yearned to know she was alright, to envision her in a place free from pain, joyfully reunited with her own mother and aunt in Heaven. All I felt in that moment, however, was an intensified yearning for her presence—her soothing voice, her infectious laughter, and the lightheartedness of our shared moments—all of which now felt like echoes in an empty hall, reverberating endlessly but never able to be grasped.

As the summer days rolled on, I found solace in the small triumphs that peppered my journey of healing. Each breakthrough with Rebecca brought me closer to newfound clarity, and for the first time, I was learning to appreciate the woman I was becoming—without the shadow of self-doubt looming over me. My struggle with body image, once a consuming fire, was now transforming into a flickering flame—a reminder of my strength rather than a source of shame.

With the changing seasons came a shift in perspective. I began to notice the rich colors of life surrounding me: the vibrant greens of the trees, the golden sunsets painting the sky, and the laughter of my family as we gathered together, honoring both my mother's memory and the lives she left behind. There was a deepening sense of connection within our family, a bond reaffirmed by shared stories of my mom's resilience and warmth. We found ways to celebrate her, from sharing her favorite recipes to participating in community events that mirrored her love for giving back.

While the absence of her physical presence created a void, I learned to listen for the whispers of her wisdom— guiding me, encouraging me, and reminding me of the power of love and laughter. On days filled with sadness, I would sit in my old room, surrounded by her photographs, and imagine her voice echoing through the walls. It felt as if our conversations were still alive, etched in time. I could almost hear her laughter ringing in my ears, coaxing me out of my sorrow and into the light.

As my therapy sessions progressed, I discovered that surrendering to my feelings didn't mean being consumed by them. It meant acknowledging my grief while also allowing joy to blossom. The burdens I once carried felt significantly lighter as I gradually embraced my worth beyond societal standards and external expectations. I began to create a vision for my future—one in which I defined success and happiness on my own terms.

I had learned to lean into my passions again, and the idea of starting my own consulting business began to bubble up from beneath the surface of my self-doubt. I envisioned a space where I could support others in navigating their careers, much like Rebecca was helping me navigate my struggles. My heart raced at the thought; it felt exhilarating, as if an ember long extinguished had suddenly been rekindled. I reached out to former colleagues and friends for guidance, reconnecting with my professional network and reigniting my love for sales leadership.

I didn't jump straight into launching a business, but I began taking small steps forward—building a website, sharpening my skills, and offering free consultations to friends and acquaintances. Each little victory grew my confidence and rekindled my drive. I wanted to be the person my mom believed I could be, and somewhere deep inside, I felt her proud smile as I took control of my narrative.

By autumn, it became evident that the seeds of healing I had planted were blossoming. One crisp evening, I joined my family for a gathering at my sister's house. We shared laughter and stories, celebrating the arrival of my mom's great-granddaughter. As I held the tiny bundle in my arms, I felt an overwhelming sense of hope wash over me. In that moment, surrounded by family, I realized that life moves inexorably forward, woven together by the threads of love, loss, and resilience.

I knew the journey of grief would ebb and flow, and there would still be days of sadness and longing ahead. But I felt fortified by the knowledge that my mother's love was forever etched in my heart, guiding me through life's uncertainties. I had embraced my past, acknowledged my grief, and allowed hope to flourish in its place.

As the last sunset of summer melted into a horizon of gray and gold, I closed my eyes and took a deep breath. I felt grounded yet free, energized yet calm. The future stretched out before me—blank pages waiting to be filled with vibrant stories of triumph, healing, and love. No longer tethered to the weight of my past, I stepped forward with fierce determination to embrace all that lay ahead.

In that moment, I understood that while my mother may have chosen her own path, her legacy continued through the footprints she left behind. With each brave step I took, I was not only discovering my own strength but also honoring her memory—a testament that love truly transcends all. With faith as my guide, I was ready to explore the adventure of life, to create my own story, and to continue growing—one day at a time.

I recalled sending her a screenshot of a meme I had found on Instagram. It read, "I wonder if my Mom can still slap me into next week? I need my paycheck early." Her response was classic: "Yes, I can. Send me your face." Those simple exchanges, filled with laughter and love, were the threads of my heart that I desperately missed.

As I sat in the quiet of my home, surrounded by her memories, a realization began to settle within me. Grief is not a linear path but a winding road filled with detours and unexpected turns—just like my mom's favorite poem. There would be days when the weight of her absence felt unbearable, and others when I could almost hear her laughter echoing through the halls of my mind. I understood now that it was okay to carry both the pain of loss and the joy of our memories.

I took a deep breath, allowing myself to embrace the complexity of my emotions. Healing would not come from rushing through grief or seeking constant validation from others, but from honoring her memory in my own way. I decided to create a space for both sorrow and gratitude—an acknowledgment that while she was gone, the love we shared would always remain.

With renewed determination, I vowed to keep her spirit alive through the stories we had shared and the laughter we had enjoyed. I would find ways to celebrate her life, to keep her close even when she was no longer physically present. Each small act of remembrance would be a step forward in my journey—a testament to the enduring bond that evolved between us.

As I looked at the pictures lining the walls and the tokens of love scattered throughout my home, I felt a flicker of hope. Perhaps healing was not about forgetting but about learning to carry her with me, transforming my grief into something that could inspire and uplift. I would not let her absence define me; instead, I would let her legacy empower me.

And so, I took a long look at the urn that held her ashes, whispering a promise into the stillness. I would live for both of us, embracing life fully, knowing that she would always be a part of my journey.